S0-BNH-067

Date Due

WASHINGTON TAPESTRY

OLIVE EWING CLAPPER

WASHINGTON TAPESTRY

Whittlesey House

McGRAW-HILL BOOK COMPANY, INC.

New York - - - - - - - - - *London*

WASHINGTON TAPESTRY

Copyright, 1946, by OLIVE EWING CLAPPER

First Printing

PUBLISHED BY WHITTLESEY HOUSE
A division of the McGraw-Hill Book Company, Inc.

Printed in the United States of America

Contents

WASHINGTON
TAPESTRY

Chapter One

A WORRIER
AT THE HELM

My husband was Raymond Clapper, newspaper reporter and radio commentator. It was his privilege to witness many of the most important events that occurred in Washington and the world during the twenty-six years from 1917 to 1944 when he worked in the central city of our government. He was personally and often intimately acquainted with the personalities that the public reads about in the newspapers.

Raymond Clapper was one of those rare reporters who kept detailed notes and descriptions of these events and these important people. This book is based upon the voluminous files he left to posterity when he was killed in an airplane crash over the Marshall Islands during the Second World War. He had intended to write a book someday that would have been his honest accounting of the historical period in which he lived.

Since he was not destined to make such a contribution, this book combines his observations as written down day by day in his notes with a few of my own memories. He is the co-author.

MY MOST VIVID MEMORIES OF WASHINGTON political life and social life started with the election of 1932.

The new candidate for President, Franklin Delano Roosevelt, invigorated the scene at the Democratic Convention that year with decision and speedy action. Yet newspapermen who knew him as Governor of New York doubted that he would make an unusual President, if elected. They liked him in a casual, but unenthusiastic manner.

They were asked, "If elected, could he deal with the crises?" Well, they doubted it, because he never had done anything spectacular. Yes, he had made a competent governor, but they weren't sure that he was big enough for the Presidency in time of crisis.

Everyone enjoyed hearing personal sidelights about Roosevelt, but overshadowing all else in every mind was the depression. The news was crowded with stories of bankers, brokers, and business men committing suicide. We bought apples from the unemployed men on street corners until we loathed the sight of red apples. We knew that the poor of many great cities were being fed in municipal soup kitchens while factory chimneys cooled, farm mortgages were foreclosed and banks failed. Truly this was a time of crisis, the total effects of which were not to be fully comprehended until a global war seared them into our consciousness.

In panic a worried people looked about for a scapegoat, and found him in Herbert Hoover, President of the United States, and now nominee of the Republican Party for a second term.

Everyone who took an active interest in the political campaign of 1932 remembers that it was marked by increasing criticism of Hoover. Nobody talked much about Franklin D. Roosevelt; the majority just railed against Hoover and jibed at him right and left. One favorite story was about a hitchhiker who made a record trip across the country, simply by holding up a sign, "If you don't give me a ride, I'll vote for Hoover."

For three long years Hoover had worried and fretted. As Admiral Grayson, physician and intimate friend of Woodrow Wilson, remarked to my husband, "Hoover is a worrier, has to read himself to sleep at night. That's not the kind of man you want for a long race." Hoover seemed unable to come to grips with the crisis. Like a drowning man, he lashed out angrily and futilely in every direction.

My husband had a forty-minute private interview with President Hoover, February 27, 1931, in which Hoover said the big job facing the country was to get out of the depression; then afterward we should make a study to see what had caused it!

He felt this was a "commodity" depression instead of a

money panic, as earlier depressions had been. By that, he meant that we had over-produced many commodities, such as coal, oil, and lumber. These excess goods couldn't move until people began to buy. The reason they didn't buy, Mr. Hoover thought, was because they were scared.

He said, "What the country needs is a good, big laugh. There seems to be a condition of hysteria. If some one could get off a good joke every ten days, I think our troubles would be over." He added, "The people have got to take care of a good many things themselves. The government can't do it. Nobody is actually starving. The hoboes, for example, are better fed than they have ever been. One hobo in New York got ten meals in one day."

Ray resisted asking, "Surely, Mr. President, you are not confusing the unemployed with hoboes, are you?"

Regardless of attempts to make Hoover see the human angle, he was obsessed with one idea. The government must not interfere with private industry, because that was social-istic. People must work their own way out of the trouble. The unemployed should be helped by private or state char-ity. He endeavored to have $300,000,000 raised by state, county, city governments, and the much-needed remainder by private contributions. He was like a man trying to plug a sieve, running from one place to another to stop up leaks which developed faster than he could run.

During this same interview, Hoover actually made the statement that if the newspapers would quit talking about unemployment our troubles would be over. His guess was that there were about four million unemployed in 1931, of which one million were being taken care of by charity.

At the end of the interview, Ray Clapper pointed out that he wished newspapermen might be given more information about what the government departments were doing to halt the depression. They could write about that and get away from talking about the depression.

Hoover growled, "We can't manufacture news for you."

Ray answered, "No, but if we can report what is being done, it would be a fine thing."

As they parted, Hoover shook his hand and said, "If you want to help, think up some good jokes."

Perhaps this paints an unfair picture of Mr. Hoover. He worked hard, he suffered much. He did influence employers to keep wages up for a long time. He scolded the bankers and said many of them should resign for mismanaging affairs. Business men also had much to answer for in taking out huge bonuses in boom years, declaring stock dividends and depleting resources, so that when the depression came they had no alternative but to cut wages.

Yet Hoover's philosophy, his shyness, and his background make it difficult for him to show bold leadership. He was caught in a relentless surge of economic chaos at home and abroad. The Machine Age was spinning the world at airplane speed. The old methods of meeting the challenge were geared to a sailing vessel. We couldn't catch up fast enough. Mr. Hoover blamed the unpaid European war debts, the press, or the breakdown in state governments; anything and everything except the real cause, which was inevitable economic revolution.

He displayed some courage when he declared a moratorium on foreign war debts. His advisers had urged for some weeks that he do so in order to ease the tense financial situation in Europe. Hoover first opposed it, believing that the people of this country would never stand for weakening on the war debts. Finally, conditions reached the point where he had to do something, and he yielded. When he announced the moratorium, it proved to be one of the most popular things he ever did. But he couldn't restore foreign trade, which was gasping in the fatal embrace of the restrictive Hawley-Smoot tariff.

Newspapermen knew that two years earlier the tide had begun to turn against Hoover. His visit to Indianapolis in 1931 gave proof of it. The crowd waiting to greet him was cold. His arrival had been timed for late afternoon, when office workers would be able to leave their offices and swell the crowd. The presidential cavalcade wound through the downtown section. The crowds were out, but there was no enthusiasm.

Some one later observed to Senator Watson that the crowd didn't seem very enthusiastic.

"They were tired," Watson said. "They had been waiting for hours, standing there on the curbs."

"But," asked a member of the party, "they weren't standing on their hands, were they?"

When Ray came to the nation's capital during the First

World War as a reporter, he often talked about Herbert Hoover, then Food Administrator in World War I. I can remember a Sunday when we walked along the sleepy old canal in Georgetown and he described Hoover sitting at his desk, puffing a cigar, calmly penciling geometrical figures on his desk pad as he talked about the grave danger of food famine. The entire Eastern seaboard had only a ten days' supply, instead of the usual thirty-day margin. Hoover feared wartime food riots, especially in large foreign centers susceptible to what he called "Bolshevik" agitation. The Food Administration was building up secret reserves of staples to forestall calamity.

Ray said he had never considered Hoover a capable political leader. As an organizer among business men, he was a wonder. He has always been a queer phenomenon—a man opposing collective bargaining and governmental control of natural resources, yet willing, as Food Czar in World War I, to commandeer the whole food supply of the nation like a dictator. But unlike dictators, he was unassuming, open to suggestion and advice.

When I asked, "Do you think Hoover will ever be President?" Ray answered, "I don't know. He comes very close to being a great man but to be a good President, he'd have to learn a lot about how the 'other half lives'—and he ought to learn what socialism really is. Then he wouldn't be afraid."

Hoover's attitude toward the farmer was that of a mining engineer, associated all his life with big business. Hoover once told Ray that some farmers were walking delegates for union labor, and that certain of their organizations were socialistic and radical. Ray was amazed at Hoover's fear as he used those two words, "socialistic" and "radical."

When Hoover won the Republican nomination in 1928, national prosperity on a grand scale lulled all fears. Shaggy-maned Senator William E. Borah was considered his only serious opponent. But the blunt, honest Borah said privately, "No man can be nominated at the Republican Convention unless he has the support of oil and other industrial interests which will control it. Can you think of any of the big interests wanting me?"

The Democrats nominated that "happy warrior" Alfred E. Smith of New York. Hoover easily defeated him, and I experienced my first bitter political disappointment. I had ardently supported Smith in violent arguments with neighbors in Washington—which did no good, of course, since none of us could vote. Washington, the District of Columbia, has no voting franchise. Its residents are governed by committees of Congress. We are political orphans and ought to hold a Boston Tea Party.

I was particularly outraged at the religious persecution of Al Smith during the campaign. The idea of pillorying a man for being a Catholic in this country which guaranteed religious freedom offended all my political liberalism.

Ray had been away traveling on campaign jaunts with Hoover part of the time and Al Smith the rest of the time. When he came home the day before election, he was dismayed to find our Ford car wearing "Vote for Al Smith" stickers. He was very angry and refused to get into the car until I took them off. He never took sides in any political campaign, believing that a reporter should keep himself untrammeled to report the unbiased news. He couldn't help personally preferring Smith to Hoover, but he leaned over backward to force himself to be neutral in his work.

The ridiculous scare over the Catholic Pope coming to rule over the United States hung over into the Hoover administration. Somes friends motored from Kansas to Washington to visit us and to see the sights. When they arrived they said they had heard that the Catholics were really running the country and Herbert Hoover. It was laughable, but we knew our Middle West. Once an idea clicks out there, many people hang on to it a long time. Haughtily Ray and I scoffed at such nonsense.

But later that morning, when we drove them down to see the White House, imagine our dismay to see a delegation of fifty Catholic priests coming out of the President's office. Our friends' eyes popped as they said, "See, we told you so." I think we failed to convince them otherwise as we explained that these men were visitors and sightseers like themselves.

But, to go back to the night of Mr. Hoover's election to the Presidency in 1928, Mr. Smith wired the usual congratulations conceding the election, as early as 10 P.M. Hoover was sitting in his home in Palo Alto listening to the returns, confident of his victory. Grumpily he remarked to a visitor,

"He should have conceded three hours ago or, better still, three months ago."

Herbert Hoover had campaigned on the slogan of "A chicken in every pot and two cars in every garage." An interesting human sidelight of history is that this phrase was coined by a newspaperman who, five years later, in 1933, hard up and unemployed, with a wife and three children to support, was in Washington begging financial assistance from other newspapermen.

Unlike Roosevelt, Hoover made friends with the greatest difficulty. His innate shyness kept his head lowered and his eyes most frequently fixed on the floor. He was inept socially. Once a charming woman sat beside him on the train at breakfast, a few days before his inauguration as President. She told him of a former college friend of his at Stanford University, who had become a bedridden invalid. He devoted all his time to collecting clippings, pictures and books about Hoover, his college hero. "It would mean everything to him," she said, "if you would send him just a brief greeting when you are in the White House."

Mr. Hoover grunted, "When you get to be President lots of people claim they used to know you." He never wrote the note.

When Hoover was inaugurated on March 9, 1929, he pledged himself to demonstrate what the engineering mind could do with the vast complex of machinery and the maelstrom of strong wills which grind at the seat of government. Trained in the policy of big business, universally regarded as one of the experts of the modern time, untrammeled by the inhibitions of the professional politician, he was the first of his kind to enter the White House. Throughout the country a feeling of expectancy developed. The government was entering a new phase.

Having served at the elbow of Presidents for eight years, Mr. Hoover moved now on sure ground as he took up the executive duties of the White House. It was as if an able vice president of a corporation had been promoted to president. There was a burst of activity such as had never been seen around the White House. He installed a telephone on his desk, hired three secretaries instead of one, enlarged the executive offices, and set to work surrounded by the paraphernalia of the efficient executive. He scrapped an old practice which required the President's signature to thousands of routine documents and authorized a clerk to affix the presidential facsimile with a rubber stamp. Public receptions, involving handshaking with several hundred and often a thousand or two callers every day, were abolished. He saw only those having important business to transact. And even with those, there was no time wasted in swapping stories.

He ordered the presidential yacht *Mayflower* laid up. Coolidge had spent many leisurely week-ends on her, but Hoover said its maintenance was too expensive. So instead he built, with the aid of Marines and Army engineers, a rustic camp on the Rapidan River in Virginia. There it would be possible to fish and still keep in close touch with the White House by direct telephone and to summon officials hastily when he wished to consult them. Fishing was his sole sport, and it is significantly one of solitude. Engineering was so deeply ingrained in him that he spoke of the bait he used for fishing as a "segment" of an angleworm.

In the White House, President Hoover never seemed to learn how to handle people or problems. He rarely changed his mind, and his vision was limited. He hesitated over decisions. On Supreme Court appointments, for example, he dallied. He was able to get Charles Evans Hughes confirmed only after a hard fight in the Senate. Another nominee—John Parker—was rejected by the Senate. When Oliver Wendell Holmes retired, Hoover was nervous. Many were urging him to appoint Cardozo of the New York Court of Appeals. It happened that Cardozo was a Jew and, since Brandeis also was, Hoover thought it would be unwise to appoint a second Jew to the Court. He also thought that with two Justices already from New York it would be a mistake to put a third one on. But Senator Borah and others insisted upon Cardozo. Finally Hoover agreed. It was one of his most widely acclaimed appointments.

An example of the political tug of war between ruthless men is the story of Hoover's appointment of Walter Edge as Ambassador to France in 1929. The battle eddied about Dwight Morrow, who was United States Minister to Mexico. He was a very able man. Hoover feared him as a rival candidate in New Jersey and wanted to keep him out of New Jersey. Friends of Morrow and big financial interests wanted Hoover to name Morrow as Secretary of the Treasury. Hoover didn't want to give him this build up. A third man, Franklin Fort, Congressman from New Jersey, who served with Hoover in the Food Administration, solved the dilemma for every one except possibly Dwight Morrow. He told Senator Edge that President Hoover would just love to appoint Mr. Morrow to the Cabinet and Senator Edge to a high diplomatic post; but, of course, Hoover could not give two such political plums to the State of New Jersey. Did Senator Edge want the diplomatic post? Or did he prefer to stay in the Senate and have Morrow put in the Cabinet? Edge grabbed the ambassadorship to France and dropped his pressure for Morrow's appointment to the Cabinet. Hoover then kept Morrow in Mexico, on the grounds he had to finish his work there.

Living up to many of the rosiest predictions of his campaign supporters, Hoover was a real executive. No President had ever worked harder. He asked only the opportunity to work. There were no afternoon naps upstairs in the White House for him, no wandering off from the worries of Washington to junket with a band of cronies around the pleasant resorts of the east, golfing by day, playing poker by night, basking in the dull banter of a crowd of good fellows, mellowing over the soft clink of ice in tall glasses. He was not the show-window President, anticking in cowboy hats before the news cameras, wasting precious time and strength by wringing endless lines of strange, sweaty hands.

But before six months had elapsed, a low rumbling sound of which the country gradually became conscious disturbed the quiet, busy efficiency of the new executive. It seemed to come from the direction of Capitol Hill, where the voice of the people is most clamorous. The Senators particularly were disturbing. They were not as docile as the average member of the House. They regarded themselves as a coordinate power of the White House. They talked too much. They were jealous of the power which they had had to yield to the President as government became more complex.

Mr. Hoover had known them before. Not only had he, as Secretary of Commerce and candidate for the Republican nomination, been hauled before Senate committees to be roughly questioned, but he had also seen what these Senators did to Woodrow Wilson and the League of Nations, which Mr. Hoover had favored. Their power was deadly then. Malevolent Senators spread their propaganda, which seeped through the country like miasma and brought catastrophe to Wilson at the height of his power. It poisoned the very air of the nation. Mr. Hoover regarded them with apprehension. He had never been of their school. Many of them—potential aspirants for the Presidency—were jealous of this outsider who had leaped over their heads to the White House. They knew he hoped to be a masterful executive and they were jealous of the power they feared he would seek to grasp. . . . All of this heightened the trepidation at the White House.

But the President and Congress rocked along without too much difficulty on the flickering gasps of prosperity until

1931, when the depression and nationwide unemployment began to build up with frightening speed.

Accompanying unemployment hysteria there was much public discussion of bootlegging and the fight to repeal the Prohibition Amendment. The bootlegging of liquor dominated all other news. The years between the ratification of the Eighteenth Amendment in 1919 and its repeal in 1933 were packed with violations of the Volstead Act, the clumsy and inadequate machinery to enforce Prohibition which worked to the advantage of the bootlegger. Speaker Longworth told of the bootlegger's child who prayed every night, "God bless mama; God bless papa; God bless Volstead."

It was so easy to get alcoholic liquor in those days. All you had to do was to telephone your favorite bootlegger who would drive up to your house, usually in a fine limousine, hand you a bottle wrapped in newspapers, as you handed him some cash. Then he'd drive off, unafraid, unconcerned.

Unable to cope with the rising panic of the depression, Mr. Hoover made a clumsy mistake when he ordered Army cavalry out to evict the bonus marchers. These war veterans had come to Washington from all over the nation by the thousands. They lobbied, picketed and did a "death" march around the Capitol, demanding cash payment of the bonus. They could not find jobs, they were penniless, hungry. I saw them marching about the White House and the Capitol Building, discouraged, hopeless remnants of that army that fought to make the world safe for democracy. President

Hoover refused to receive them or to talk to them. They were not really terrifying in their makeshift clothes. They camped out on government property; some of them even built houses from crates and tin cans. Hoover was supposedly an outdoors man himself. Perhaps if he had joined them, or even talked genially with them, they would have consented to return to their homes. But he would not receive them.

Suddenly, after Congress voted them money for transportation back to their homes but refused to vote them the bonus, a policeman was killed in a street incident. At once troops from Fort Meyer were called out, shacks were burned, American citizens were driven about at the point of bayonets. The sky was red as we drove out to see the burning hovels. Newspapermen were pushed around, ordered off the scene. It was very hard to feel easy in your heart as you witnessed the United States Army moving against United States citizens.

Hoover's press relations were deplorable. Newspapermen tore their hair over the many fights they had with President Hoover and his press secretaries. Ray was constantly in hot water over stories written by his staff, to which the White House or some government official objected. Every newspaper office had similar trouble.

In addition to his public fears, Mr. Hoover had a severe personal fright, one summer night at dinner in the White House. He looked up from his dinner plate to see a strange man walk through the entrance hall and enter the East Room. Hastily Hoover called the secret service men on

duty. They rushed to the East Room, surrounded and arrested the stranger. He was a nice-looking man, hatless, but
dressed in dinner clothes, with a brief case under his arm.
He said he was a lawyer from a midwestern state, come to
Washington to appear before a court for a client. It was his
first visit to Washington, and he wanted to see points of
interest—such as the White House. He had been busy all
day, hadn't been able to see the White House during the
regular sightseeing hours. He had decided to see it that
night. Finding the gates open, he had walked into the driveway, nodded to the policeman there.

At that time, the city police were charged with guarding
the grounds; the secret service took up jurisdiction at the
White House doors—a divided responsibility. This night,
the secret service man at the door saw the policeman at the
gate greet the caller and assumed this was an expected
guest, or perhaps a State Department aide coming to see the
President on business. It was a very hot night, all the doors
were open. The secret service man nodded good evening,
too, and the man walked into the White House, past
Hoover's astonished gaze. He inspected the famous gold
piano in the East Room and was gazing at Martha Washington's portrait when arrested. His brief case bore out his iden-
tity, and he was released after investigation.

But the episode so terrified the President that he called
the secret service chief to the White House that same night.
Negotiations were begun at once, giving full responsibility

to the Secret Service for guarding the White House and the grounds as well.

By September, 1931, Hoover was insisting that although one million people would be starving that winter, conditions were improving. He urged that $200,000,000 be raised privately for relief. He said that the United States could be run either as an outright capitalist country or as an outright Communist country—but it couldn't be run by a mixture of the two. Federal help for the unemployed would be half communistic, he seemed to think. He would not dream of direct help to aid the starving or of pump priming to make jobs for the unemployed so they could begin consumer buying, which might start the wheels of industry anew.

Yet behind the scenes, Congressional members were using government funds to amplify their personal incomes. In 1932 Ray wrote a series of stories about graft in small and large ways by Senators, members of the House of Representatives, and by executives in public departments of the government who were lining their private pockets at the expense of the taxpayer. He told of nepotism, that well-known racket of putting relatives on the public payroll; of luxurious junkets and padded expense accounts during a time when millions of citizens were out of work.

So successful was the series that a publisher asked him to write a book, which was called *Racketeering in Washington* and published in 1933. Typical of the indictments in the book was the sad case of Senator Smith W. Brookhart, horny-handed son from the rich soil of Iowa who pyramided his senatorial privileges into a lucrative income.

Born in a log cabin, life had been hard for Smith Brookhart. He had fought the poor farmers' battles in Iowa; and, when he came to the U.S. Senate, his speeches were full of bitterness against big business, Wall Street interests and railroads. Yet he loaded up his payroll with himself and his family to the tune of $25,000 a year.

Brookhart also was subjected to a withering attack for his part in the mileage grab in 1930. He had been absent from the Senate for 49 working days while making Chautauqua speeches at fees estimated at $200 to $300 a day. He was drawing $30 a day senatorial pay. While galloping about the country on the barn-storming trip, he did a perfect job of timing his schedule in order to get back to Washington in time to collect his railroad mileage for the Senate's special session. He did not forget that he had an allowance coming to him of 40 cents a mile from his home in Iowa to Washington, D.C., even though he never attended the session at all. On the afternoon of the last day, he had the Senate Clerk make a notation in the *Congressional Record* that he had appeared in his Senate seat that day. With the record thus made straight, though he had been in town hardly an hour, he hustled to the window of the disbursing officer, made out his mileage claim and collected $416 in railroad mileage for a trip home which, even if he had taken it, would have cost an actual fare (with a lower berth) of only $97.48.

The book, filled with such exposures, had only a mild

sale because it appeared when the New Deal was being ushered in and the depression was heavy upon the book-buying public. Its main effect was to alarm official Washington into a more responsible attitude toward the public treasury. Nepotism defeated many members of Congress in the November elections of 1932.

I think Ray was tremendously impressed throughout all his writing on nepotism by the way Senators and Representatives took this punishment. His dispatches were painful reading to many of them; avalanches of critical letters poured in upon them from their constituents. Yet, to their credit, they never whimpered nor were they bitter toward Ray. Of course, they didn't like it, but they took it as good sports.

Shortly thereafter, on Capitol Hill one day, Ray met Ernie Smoot, son of Senator Reed Smoot. Ray, having written reams of devastating exposure of Senator Smoot's nepotistic dynasty, was not prepared for Ernie Smoot's enthusiastic greeting, "I want to thank you for the fine write-up you gave my father. He appreciated it and all of us did." It was like the time George Harvey, editor of the Washington *Post*, ran a series of editorials tearing the hide off Senator J. Hamilton Lewis of Illinois. He heard nothing from Lewis. The editorials finally stopped. A few days later, Harvey received a note from Senator Lewis thanking him for his "kindly" mention of him and noting that he had seen nothing for the last few days. "Have I done anything to offend you that you should stop writing about me?"

A Worrier at the Helm

Meanwhile the country stood still on dead center. The bitterness built up against Herbert Hoover. We were glad and hopeful when Franklin Roosevelt flew out to Chicago to accept the Democratic nomination for President and began to feel much like the editorial writer in the London *Economist*, who wrote, much later in 1936:

"The people will forgive the bold experimentalist his occasional errors in gratitude for his strenuous good intentions. They will never tolerate the cautious pedant who waits before moving to be sure that every last detail of his plan is approved by the orthodox and consequently seems never to move at all. Politics is the art of the possible, not the science of the ideal. It is the Roosevelts who, with all their faults, inconsistencies, become, and deserve to become, the great statesmen."

Action we needed, and action is what we got.

Chapter Two

THE MIRACLE
MEN MOVE IN

IT IS CURIOUS THAT THE REPUBLICAN CAM-
paign of 1932 never degenerated into an attack on Roosevelt's invalidism. Once some photographs of Roosevelt being
helped out of a car were sent to Hoover, with the suggestion
that circulation of them might help the Republican campaign
—but they were never used. Creditable, also, was the sportsmanship of photographers, reporters and editors, who refrained from picturing or emphasizing the physical handicap.

Franklin Roosevelt had to wear very uncomfortable, in-
tricate steel braces on both legs extending to his hips. To sit
down he had to keep both feet stretched out until he could
release the mechanism at the knees. To rise the braces had
to be tightened to hold the support rigid. This was always
painful to him physically and psychologically. On two public
occasions that I know of his braces gave way under him and
he fell. The press refrained from ever mentioning it and in
the public mind he always stood as a powerful, commanding
figure of a man.

Once in 1939 I rode up with him in the elevator in the

The Miracle Men Move In

White House. He sat in his wheel chair. He was tired and feverish. As I stood above him he looked so crumpled, broken and invalided I could hardly restrain the tears. For the first time I realized that here was a man who fought a gallant battle with himself every day.

Roosevelt won the 1932 election with a seven million popular majority. President Hoover twice invited him to the White House for consultation as the money panic began in real earnest during the three months between Roosevelt's election and inauguration. Banks crashed only here and there, at first. Then runs on banks started, and the crashes crescendoed into national panic. Banker and stock market suicides were daily occurrences.

Yet, in Washington, the carpenters building the wooden inaugural parade stands—the first work they had had in months—went on strike for more pay and staged a slowdown!

Three weeks before inauguration Washington's nerves were raw. Democrats, out of office since 1918, poured into town hoping for appointments, and the poor, defeated Republicans shivered as moving vans signalized their plunge back into the chill of private life. Few politicians emulated the sturdy example of Secretary of the Navy Adams who, when asked what he was going to do after the Democrats were inaugurated, said, "I'm going back to Boston and mind my own business."

The Senate got terribly upset when David Barry, Sergeant-at-Arms of the Senate, printed an article in the *New*

Outlook which opened with this blow: "Contrary to popular belief, there are not many crooks in Congress; that is, out-and-out grafters, or those who are willing to be such. There are not many Senators or Representatives who sell their votes for money, and it is pretty well known who those few are." Furiously, the Senate started to investigate Mr. Barry but, after Mr. Barry quoted two of its own members in support of his assertions, the august Senators hushed up the matter.

Such nervous spells have come over Washington since it was founded. They provide great fun for the spectators. Newspapermen, knowing that the taxpayers must pay four billion dollars a year to keep the circus going here, are inclined to think often that the show is not good enough.

Newspapermen, trying to dope out Roosevelt's Cabinet appointments, did not even speculate on Harold Ickes, Republican Progressive of Chicago, as Secretary of the Interior. He had closed his law office and wanted to go into public service. He wanted to be Indian Commissioner or, if that were too ambitious, he shyly admitted to his friend, Newton Jenkins, that he'd be willing to be Assistant Indian Commissioner. Mr. Jenkins said, "Why not aim high, Harold, and be Secretary of the Interior?" Jenkins began sending telegrams to the incoming President, had other friends write to build up a fire for Ickes' appointment. When Roosevelt reached his deadline on naming his Cabinet, he had been so bombarded by Republican and Progressive Senators and friends of Ickes, he suddenly called Ickes and appointed him.

A week before Roosevelt's inauguration I was called one day to the telephone. My husband said, "Honey, don't be too alarmed but I hear that our bank is folding. When it closes at 2 P.M. today, it will never open again. I was just tipped off. You have fifteen minutes to get there and draw out enough cash to run the house a couple of weeks. I hate to take advantage of the situation and this tip-off, but we've got to think of food for our children. Don't get panicky and don't spread the rumor. Maybe this is a false alarm. But I'm afraid by the end of the week all the banks in the country will be closed. The United Press has ordered me to draw out enough for our payroll for two weeks, which I am now rushing out to do. Keep your shirt on, don't ask questions, just do as I tell you. Good-bye."

When I got to the bank, the blanched faces and pale lips of the tellers were confirmation enough. I knew I should act quickly and take out all we had, but it seemed so unfair that I drew out only a couple of hundred dollars. I simply couldn't believe our bank was failing. I forgot about the large check for the half-yearly payment on our house that had not cleared the bank. So, to our losses, I had to add several hundred dollars more when, the next morning, the familiar bank doors were locked against the milling crowd.

Inauguration day, March, 1933, dawned cloudy and raw. I had a ticket for a seat on the Capitol Plaza, right in front of the House wing of the Capitol. My children, accompanied by a friend, had been invited to view the parade from a balcony of the Willard Hotel overlooking Pennsylvania Avenue.

We were cold and gray as we waited for the inauguration ceremonies to begin. With a friend, I stood up on the board seat in front of the House side of the Capitol as Chief Justice Charles Evans Hughes administered the oath to the solemn man who launched at once into an eloquent challenge that stirred us to tears of relief. In measured, confident tones Roosevelt told us:

"This great nation will endure as it has endured, will revive and will prosper. Let me affirm that the only thing we have to fear is fear itself."

With burning words, he charged that the "money changers" had no vision and had fled their "high seats in the temple of our civilization." He pledged action in a fighting speech that thrilled us into forgetfulness of the cold. Our shivers were those of amazement, of inspiration, of new courage. Here was a leader, here was hope. Cheers rose from a hundred thousand throats.

When he finished, we joined the pellmell dash of thousands down the hill to find our place to watch the parade. We couldn't get on a street car or bus or into a taxi. We decided to walk to the Willard Hotel, many blocks away. The parade was already beginning to pass the Willard as we finally coaxed a policeman to let us cross the street to the hotel where we joined our children and friends in a suite. The parade of 18,000 marching men and women was a glamorous pageant to thrill the depressed hearts of five hundred thousand visitors.

The day Franklin Roosevelt was inaugurated Raymond Clapper was manager of the United Press Bureau in Washington. It was a busy day for him. As I write I have before me his assignment sheet for his staff covering all angles of that exciting day. His general instructions were:

"Pump copy in short and fast. Don't let it pile up in your lap.

"Strive for speed and accuracy—human interest—quotes —names—color. Be sure before you let it go. Every man should be alert for the unexpected. At the first sign of any trouble, get the office quick. Don't wait for details.

"Every man should realize that there is greater danger of an attempt against the life of the President and other prominent persons than on any other story we ever covered here. Be prepared in your own mind at all times just how you will get the office. Two persons will be with the new President at all times. They should know where the nearest telephone is. Get it open at the first sign of anything untoward."

What a story that 1933 inauguration was!

The New York *Times* the following morning carried a front-page story datelined Berlin which had little significance for us at the time. It told of another election climaxed by bonfires and torchlight parades of great patriotic fervor, as the Nationalist-Socialist party took control of Germany. Adolf Hitler, amidst acclaim, became dictator. The story significantly said, "There were no counter-demonstrations from the opposition. They were 'verboten,' for this is a one-way election. Nor, late tonight, despite the dire predictions sent to the outside world, had any serious disturbance been reported. All that is over, for what is the use of inviting inevitable and overwhelming reprisals when all the authority and all the weapons are monopolized by the other side?"

Mr. Roosevelt gave the banks a four-day "holiday," as he expressed it—psychologically a much better word than "moratorium." He moved with speed to set the nation's crippled economics into healing splints. We watched his startling innovations with wonder and enthusiasm.

He showed immediately that he knew how to deal with the press by summoning the chiefs of the four press associations to the White House the second evening he was in office (Sunday, March 5) to explain to them what he was doing in closing the banks, so that they would be able to interpret properly the stories that went out to the jittery nation. The President received them in the upstairs study. He was in great good humor. Ray was given a telephone across from the study and allowed to telephone a lead of the story to his office, although the full text was not released until eleven that night. As Ray dictated, Roosevelt waited to go on the air with his first fireside chat to the nation. All was quiet, calm, congenial as he spoke into the microphones. Mrs. Roosevelt and the President's mother sat nearby. A little black terrier named Scottie hopped about.

The Miracle Men Move In

Roosevelt was demonstrating by these two actions—his careful explanations to the press and his fireside talk to the people of the country—his democratic attitude toward his position. If ever a man had a setup for dictatorship, Roosevelt had it those early weeks and months. Business men in their panic were begging the executive to take over everything. Congress was putty in his hands, and public opinion was heavily behind him. They would have applauded anything he did. In later years, he was accused again and again of wanting to become a dictator. At that perilous moment in our history, he could have been one with almost unanimous consent.

There were no firing lines or pitched battles, but, between March 4 and April 1, a revolution took place in the United States. We were not able to comprehend it all at once but, in seven days, a new age burst upon us. We changed our whole concept toward economic ills. The Federal Government would not allow men to starve and, furthermore, it would attempt to regulate a vast nation's problems to uphold the hands of the "forgotten man."

So stupendous was the salvaging effort that Secretary of the Interior Ickes alone had undertaken to spend in less than a year a sum equal to three dollars for every minute since the birth of Christ. Christ was born a few million more than a billion minutes ago, and the Government planned to spend our way back to prosperity—approximately three billion, three hundred million dollars. It was nothing short of financing a war!

The Miracle Men Move In

One of the stories going the rounds about the New Deal was apropos the expenditure of large sums for relief. It was told by Governor Talmadge of Georgia. A Georgia cracker who was hard up wrote to Washington and addressed his letter to "The Lord, Washington, D.C." The letter went to the dead letter office. They opened it there and found in it a request for $200. After reading the hard luck story, the employees took up a collection. They raised $100 and enclosed it with a note signed: "From the Lord."

A week later, a letter came back from him, again addressed to the Lord. It said: "Dear Lord: Your letter received. Thank you for answering my prayer. But when the letter got here $100 was missing. The next time, don't let any of those New Dealers fool with your mail."

At his first press conference Roosevelt said there would be no limit on questions the newspapermen could ask. The White House "spokesman" of the Coolidge administration was abandoned, as was the silence of President Hoover, who seldom departed from his prepared statement. Sometimes, Roosevelt said, he would not answer their questions because he would not always know the answers, or for other reasons he might not think it wise to comment. However, he was not to be directly quoted unless a transcript of his remarks was given to them by the White House. When he spoke "off the record," everything he said must be observed as confidential and must not be revealed to friends or even to the news editors. He never answered an "if" question, he said, but he would try to give them background.

This attitude was such an advance over press-coverage allowed by former Presidents that the 125 men who swarmed into the oval room for that first press conference listened and were grateful for the valuable information Roosevelt gave. They all laughed at a quip or two of his and spontaneously burst into handclapping when the conference ended.

Congress remained in session and at executive bidding, laws and regulations tumbled out for banking and the stock market; a vast program of public works to clear slums, develop sewerage systems, develop waterways; the National Recovery Act; the Agricultural Adjustment Act—a thousand schemes to start the wheels of prosperity again.

Although the President spearheaded these new moves, a new type of government official appeared with the innovations. Rexford Guy Tugwell, Adolf Berle, Raymond Moley, Harry Hopkins, Henry Wallace, Hugh Johnson and Donald Richberg were among those who brought a sense of planning, of foresight and of comprehension of the vastness of economic relationships wholly unknown before. We called them "braintrusters." At first, they seemed like Don Quixotes tilting at windmills. Everyone laughed at them. But Ray didn't laugh because so much they said made sense if the American ideal was to be saved.

Sometimes in those early days of the New Deal it seemed as if there really were magicians around pulling white rabbits out of a hat. A friend of ours called on Henry Wallace, Secretary of Agriculture. He saw something dart from under the desk and dash across the room. He looked again and blinked his eyes in astonishment. Sure enough it was as he thought . . . a white rabbit.

"Don't tell me, Mr. Secretary," he said, "that all of these stories I've been hearing about you folks pulling rabbits out of hats are true!"

Wallace chuckled and replied, "That white rabbit belongs to my boy. He wanted me to bring it down to have our veterinarians check up on him."

A great many Democrats were dissatisfied with the New Deal. They formed organizations such as the Liberty League, but they did not leave the Party. Some New Dealers wished they would and recalled the story of a Dartmouth lad who wrote to the President of Dartmouth saying the courses were too hard and added a postscript: "I wish I had went to Yale." The President of Dartmouth forwarded the letter to his friend, the President of Yale, with this notation: "I wish he had, too."

Al Smith and others through the years who disagreed with Roosevelt's policies clung to the Party, however. They were in the position of a man at a southern revival meeting. The preacher exhorted sinners to come forward. He fixed one particular seedy listener with a glittering eye and shouted: "Have you made your peace with God?"

The prospect looked puzzled for a moment and then replied: "There ain't yet been no open breach."

I met Dr. Tugwell, Assistant Secretary of Agriculture, braintruster and glamor boy of the New Deal, at a supper party at the Ray Tuckers' house. He was very handsome—

wavy, iron-gray hair, deep gray eyes behind movie-star eyelashes. Surprisingly shy, his manner seemed mocking and chilly. That night I was feeling especially gay and partyish. Glibly, I said to him,

"Dr. Tugwell, I have an agricultural problem upon which I'd like your advice. I know you are an economist and not a farmer, so maybe you'll have to send me a bulletin from the department instead of answering it yourself."

He blushed and I boldly proceeded.

"We have several young pear trees in our garden. This is the first year they have borne any pears. I've hung over them and watched the little pears grow into big ones, ripening in the sun. But yesterday, just after I decided we would have several beautiful pears to eat in a few days, the squirrels discovered them. Apparently, they like green pears for they take a running leap into those little trees and devour the pears. What can I do about that?"

He listened to my silly question, gave me a pained look and walked away. I felt utterly chagrined and foolish. Apparently, Dr. Tugwell wanted to be serious, even at parties.

Later, when I was seated on the divan with a plate of supper balanced on my knee, he came to sit beside me to eat. I decided to be very serious and converse about weighty topics. Before I could launch into one, Dr. Tugwell shyly, quietly, with a warm twinkle in his eyes, said,

"I've been thinking over your problem of the squirrels in the pear trees, and I think I have a solution. I have always understood that squirrels relish nuts. Why don't you plant a 'nurtz tree,' and maybe they would leave your pears alone."

I always thought of his delightful, quiet humor as big business men and members of Congress pilloried him in the following months, accusing him of fantastic ideas, making fun of his housing schemes, his broad economic planning. Everything he tried to do they labeled "Communistic." He described himself as a Liberal and said, "Liberals would like to rebuild the railroad station while the trains are running; radicals prefer to blow up the station and forego service until the new structure is built."

Tugwell, a scholar, had a scientific approach to the economic and social problems of the day, but he recognized the question mark in human behavior and never expected a millennium. He had an utter scorn for politics and politicians. No wonder. For example, if he worked with great ardor on a Pure Food and Drug Bill, or any much-needed reform, he would discover that feeling against him was strong enough to defeat anything he tried to do. His most valuable contribution was the education he gave his opponents and the public. Today, many of his ideas seem reasonable and almost conservative. A very hard worker, he never spared himself. He weathered a deep public distrust and paved the way for sensible, planned experiments in political science.

His approach to government was that it "must do what we expect of it, or it must be changed so that it will." He said:

"As individuals, we are apt to ride in airplanes with horse-and-buggy ideas in our heads. And our Government has done

the same thing. It has attempted to function in a world
which has long since outgrown it. All the prejudices and
shibboleths which survive in people's heads seem to crystal-
lize in government—perhaps because, very rightly, we think
of it as somehow sacred. But it will not stay sacred long if it
is set apart from change in a changing world. It will simply
become atrophied and obsolete, and will either be ignored
or contemptuously brushed aside by those in the community
who have important affairs afoot which they desire shall not
be interfered with."

Dr. Tugwell was by no means as dour and unapproachable
as he was pictured. He did like to have fun.

I sat beside him at dinner at the Soviet Embassy one night.
It was a huge dinner with 96 guests seated. The table
stretched through the enormous dining room, through a long
hall and halfway through Ambassador Troyanovsky's study
in one continuous line. The invitation was for dinner at nine,
a late hour for Americans to eat. No cocktails were served.
Starved, we trooped out to the beautiful, luxurious table,
found our places midway of the long table and, in Russian
fashion, drank in one gulp the tiny glasses of vodka as soon
as we were seated. The fiery drink lit that audience like a
firecracker. At once hilarity rippled up and down the endless table. Dr. Tugwell turned to me and said as he picked
a pecan from the nut dish, "Can you see Madame Troyanovsky at the end of the table way down there?"

"No, I can't see her so far away amid such masses of flowers. Can you?"

"No, I can't either. But I'll bet you after that glass of vodka I can throw this pecan so far and straight that I can hit her." He let go with the nut and, laughing, I, too, sent one down the table. We didn't hit Madame Troyanovsky, but, later that night, a distinguished dowager in the lady's room frowned as she extracted a pecan from her bosom.

This dinner occurred about a year or more after our government recognized the Stalin regime and exchanged ambassadors with the Union of Soviet Socialist Republics.

Prior to the United States' recognition of Russia, one of our assistant secretaries of State told Ray that our government had more complete and up-to-date information on Russia than any other government. But the trouble was that the Soviet Union had nothing in common with the other governments of the world; they didn't think in the same terms on business contracts or any of the ordinary working arrangements between individuals and governments. We had no common meeting ground at all. It was like trying to bring a grizzly bear and an eagle to an understanding. The problem had three aspects: economic, political, social.

In a roundabout yet highly interesting way, the wheels were set going in 1933 for United States recognition of the Soviet Union. President Roosevelt sent a message to Boris Skirsky, unofficial representative of the Russians in the United States. . . . Would Skirsky please find out if a message to Kalinin, President of the Soviets, would be favorably received in Moscow? The Soviets replied by cable to Skirsky that it would be welcomed. Roosevelt then cabled

The Miracle Men Move In

Kalinin his willingness to receive an official of the Soviet to talk about an exchange of diplomats. The cumbersome interchange of cables continued with poor Skirsky the middleman. Kalinin asked Skirsky to sound out Roosevelt to see if his contemplated reply—naming Maxim Litvinoff, Commissar of Foreign Affairs, as the man who would come over to talk over the whole matter—was satisfactory. That suited President Roosevelt. Skirsky cabled an O.K., and soon the official cable went through to the White House, naming Litvinoff.

All that double trouble just to get the wheels moving!

While he was working on Soviet recognition, President Roosevelt had Cardinal O'Connell at the White House, quieting the Catholics to clear the way for recognition—a very wise political move.

We had known and felt affection for the Boris Skirskys. When, after the arrival of the Ambassador and Madame Troyanovsky, we received one of the coveted huge engraved invitations, with hammer and sickle legend on it, to a reception at the long-closed Russian Embassy on Sixteenth Street, I eagerly awaited the evening. I walked up the red-carpeted stairs into the gorgeous drawing rooms of the famous Pullman house—long occupied by the ambassadors of Czarist Russia. The buffet was the most lavish I had ever seen. Cocktail bars flourished in rooms on every floor. The crush of people, the hilarity, the elegance was a far cry from the Volga Boatman song. It was a great party in true capitalistic style. I thought often of it when I was in Russia later.

The Miracle Men Move In

Franklin and Eleanor Roosevelt had lived three months in the White House when they gave their first enormous evening party for the press. It was a steaming June night. Newspapermen hate to dress up, especially in stiff black dinner clothes. There had been lots of discussion over what they should wear this night. Had they only known that the President would wear a white silk suit, bowing to tradition only by wearing a black tie, many of them would have worn more comfortable clothes.

I remember the party best for a singular kindness President Roosevelt bestowed upon a lonely young lady who seemed to have no one with whom to dance. He said to her, "Go out onto the terrace, pick out the best-looking man there and tell him, on my command, to dance with you." Imagine the surprise of handsome Duane Wilson, newspaper reporter for the United Press Association, when the young lady walked up and said, "The President commands you to dance with me." After the waltz, she led him back to the President, who looked Wilson up and down and said, "Well, he looks all right to me. You made a good choice."

Altogether, it was a very lively party—"The liveliest the White House has seen since Nick Longworth and Alice were married here," the President said.

The first time we dined at the White House after the Roosevelts came to live there, we were invited most informally. One of Mrs. Roosevelt's secretaries telephoned, "The President and Mrs. Roosevelt would like you and Mr. Clapper to come in for informal supper Sunday night—bacon and scrambled eggs, you know."

I assumed it was to include a large group of newspaper people and expected to sit near some well-known friend; but, when we entered the front door, one aide took our wraps and another said, "Mrs. Clapper, supper will be served in the main dining room tonight. You will be seated on the President's left, Mrs. Moffett on his right." My mind was instantly in a flutter about what in the world I could talk about to this great, new President. I said: "Heavens, how awful," to the shocked presidential aide. My husband came to my rescue by adding, "She'll get along all right . . . I've never known her to be unable to talk."

This Sunday evening I wasn't feeling glamorous, for I wore an unexciting black dress and owned no fine jewelry to relieve it. We walked into the Blue Room, where Mrs. Roosevelt received us. President Roosevelt was always seated in the dining room, and the guests greeted him as they went to their dinner places. We sat at an oval table and, instead of a large party, we numbered only eleven altogether.

When I saw the glamorous Mrs. Moffett, wife of the Housing Administrator, in a glittering blue sequin evening gown bedecked with some of the world's finest sapphires, I ceased to worry about conversing with the President. I was sure he'd never turn in my direction. But as I sat down after shaking his hand, he turned at once to me and said: "Ray has not been looking very well lately. Don't you think he is working too hard?"

The Miracle Men Move In

Now if there is one subject a wife can always talk about, it is her husband's health. In no time at all I was chattering away about all kinds of things—laughing, telling jokes as though we were old friends. The President offered me a cigarette from a crumpled pack he pulled from his pocket and said, "Senator McAdoo dropped in to tell me good-bye today."

"Where is he going?" I asked.

"To California," he answered, whereupon we both burst out laughing as he continued, "No, not to marry Shirley Temple."

The joke was that Senator McAdoo had just married a charming lady many years his junior, furnishing the nation with the usual amusement when an elderly man takes a youthful wife.

When we quieted down, he said he had often wondered who thought up jokes and marveled at the speed with which they traveled about the country. He said a wisecrack or joke spoken in New York often reached San Francisco in a matter of hours, and he surmised that they must be sent by telegram or on stockbrokers' tickers.

After supper we went upstairs to the family living room. The President and his secretary, Miss Marguerite Le Hand, retired to his study to work. Mr. and Mrs. Moffett left to catch a train. I was so fascinated with Mrs. Roosevelt's conversation that I failed to realize that I was the only other woman present and therefore was the one upon whom devolved the responsibility of making the first move to go home. I was so used by this time to waiting until a ranking lady decided to break up the party, that I relaxed with irresponsibility. As the evening went on pleasantly, I hung on Mrs. Roosevelt's every word until even I became conscious of the hour and wondered why no one made a move to say good-night. Suddenly I realized that I was the ranking lady, there being none other present except the First Lady. I bolted out of my chair while Mrs. Roosevelt was in the middle of a sentence and said, "Oh, we must go home." She looked astonished at my rudeness, as well she might, finished her sentence, and we left—the remaining gentlemen close on our heels. I was glad to see it was only ten forty-five as we drove off.

With the Roosevelt administration making big news every hour on the hour, newspapermen had to pick and choose from the deluge of news. A Washington correspondent had to be a gold expert on Monday, a farm expert on Tuesday, an inflation expert on Wednesday, never forgetting—as Ray said—to put in a few scoopfuls of political gossip to salt the alphabetical soup. Washington was a newspaperman's paradise, with a page one story around every corner. The best copy of all, however, was that refreshing new man in the White House. Ray estimated that newsmen were about 75 percent in favor of the New Deal program, but they were 95 percent for Roosevelt by 1935.

And to keep them busy there were investigations galore, such as the investigation into "the power trust," through

which—as Tom Stokes says in *Chip Off My Shoulder*—
"The country learned how low some of the idols of the
golden era of prosperity, the supposed Big Men of America,
could stoop in their mad chase for profits . . . learned how
lightly they regarded corruption of politics to achieve their
ends."

The banking investigation intrigued me. Here in the "million dollar" Caucus Room of the Senate, we watched the
money changers driven from the temples of public opinion.
It shook Washington as nothing had since the Teapot Dome
disclosures. J. P. Morgan, reigning prince of American
finance, was found to be paying no income taxes just as Congress was about to raise the average person's income tax. To
our dismay, we learned that the bookkeeping of the mighty
Morgan banking house was free from regulation and exam-
ination.

This hearing was superdrama. Under four glittering chan-
deliers sat Morgan the magnificent, calm, smiling, wiping
a bead of perspiration away as a totally different kind of a
man, Ferdinand Pecora, swarthy Italian-American counsel
for the Senate Banking Committee, questioned and probed. I
can think of no other scene that presented a better spectacle
of human contrasts. J. P. Morgan—aristocratic Episcopalian,
with steam yachts, hunting lodges in Scotland, so haughty a
ruler of America that he had ordered news photographers
from his sight in the past—was brought low by a struggling
lawyer who rose up from a sweatshop.

Yes, we saw a revolution as Morgan lost many special

privileges, as did other leading financiers including Albert H. Wiggin of the Chase National Bank, Charles E. Mitchell of the National City Bank of New York, Clarence Dillon of Dillon, Read and Company, the Van Sweringen brothers of Cleveland, and Samuel Insull.

With headlines and parades, the Federal Government sought to regulate into cooperation business, industry, and labor. Swiftly on the wings of a blue eagle came the National Recovery Act.

I could never quite comprehend what all the noise was about in the NRA. Perhaps that buccaneer, Hugh Johnson, who administered it, made too great a fuss and too many enemies; or perhaps the New Deal just tried too quickly to change our ancient customs. Hugh Johnson was gruff and tough, with large, round, hard-blue eyes which could become as flinty as a banker's; a jaw that snapped with the impact of a sledgehammer. His hard-boiled language was that of his early cavalry years, sprinkled with sulphur. His pet phrases were: "You guys," "cut out that guff," "bunk," "hooey," "chiselers." He had a rough humor. In the early stages of the NRA, when industry was fearful that he was about to strap it in a strait jacket, Johnson smiled and said:

"We're going to be reasonable. I'm not going to try to put everybody in a Procrustean bed." He was recalling the evildoer of mythology who had an iron bedstead on which he tied all travelers who fell into his hands. If they were shorter than the bed, he stretched their arms and legs to make them fit it. If they were longer, he hacked off a portion.

The Miracle Men Move In

At any rate, Ray explained to me what the government wanted to do, about as follows. . . .

The NRA covered practically every line of manufacturing and commercial activity from brassieres to boilers, from pretzels to pumps, from lace curtains to steam shovels, from hairdressers to garbage collectors, from the giant steel, automobile, and coal industries to the manufacturers of nose rings for hogs and the makers of mopstick handles.

Minute rules were laid down in the codes governing all industry. Wage scales were described in detail. Hours of labor were fixed. In many instances the number of hours that machinery could be used was limited, so that manufacturers could not overload the market by running their iron men both day and night.

Ray told me about the case of a small sweater factory in a certain New England village. It had been losing business because it could not meet the prices of competitors and was about to close down. The owner called in his employees and described his desperate situation. He proposed that if they would accept another 20 percent wage cut—and there had been other reductions before—he would try to carry on. With that reduction in his manufacturing costs, he believed he could take his sweaters to New York and undersell the market. He did undersell the market and obtained enough orders to keep running full time for three months. He took these orders away from other sweater factories in nearby communities; and they, for lack of orders, had in a number of instances to close down.

The Miracle Men Move In

This was a good illustration of the effects of cutthroat competition which were being similarly felt in many industries. Reckless price cutting of this kind was driving one business after another into the hands of the sheriff. In the process, additional persons were being thrown out of work. Wages of those who managed to hold their jobs were ground still lower as employers strove to reduce costs in order to get under prices of competitors. Such desperate struggles reduced the principle of free competition to a ghastly farce, and to a form of slow economic suicide for all.

Roosevelt and his advisers were convinced that the old order of unrestrained competition had broken down and could never be restored. They sought to build through NRA a hybrid form of industrial self-government, under the supervisory hand of the Federal Government.

But it didn't work and, amidst a general breakdown of the scheme, Hugh Johnson resigned and the Supreme Court declared the NRA unconstitutional. Public opinion decided our capitalistic system worked better under its own steam, without any "meddling" by the government. But I am inclined to agree with Donald Richberg, counsel for the NRA, writing in his book *The Rainbow:*

"The foundation work for a permanent structure of better cooperative relations in planning and advancing the industrial activities of the United States was, however, the major undertaking of the NRA that may yet have far-reaching consequences. What was attempted, what difficulties were encountered, what useful mechanisms were invented and what experimental efforts promised increasing gains out of further development—these are matters worthy of a careful review and must furnish the basis for future constructive action."

Like everyone else we found amusement in the tales about Hugh Johnson. We used to see him at Bethany Beach, Delaware, in later years, robustly swimming in the sea or equally robustly swimming in alcohol. He became a newspaper columnist, famous for his pungent, earthy phrases; and with Heywood Broun, Westbrook Pegler, Ernie Pyle and Raymond Clapper created an editorial diet that made the columnists of the Scripps-Howard papers famous throughout the land.

But the personality from NRA that we know and love best is Donald R. Richberg. He became my husband's dearest friend. Don was a Teddy Roosevelt Progressive in his youth, gave up a profitable law practice in Chicago to come to Washington at Franklin Roosevelt's request to help in the early New Deal days. He was very close to that throne, and many of Roosevelt's finest speeches bear the imprint of Donald Richberg's facile pen. Intelligent, witty, and practical, his devotion to the problem of making democracy work should have kept him at Roosevelt's side. But Tom Corcoran, member of the Presidential secretariat and for a time an intimate friend of Roosevelt, was jealous and eased the President away from many of his wisest advisers. Don would have sacrificed health and wealth to have served, but he was too honest and forthright to fight backstage intrigue. He took up

a successful law practice in Washington and displayed a remarkable ability to "live happily ever after."

At home in Washington or on the beach under striped umbrellas, like every one else, we talked much of the New Deal.
We felt its evolution had a simple philosophy behind it,
which could be summarized into one sentence: profits having
been the sole aim of business in the past, this profit motive
needed to be subordinated to the welfare of the whole people
through government control.

Norman Thomas called this state capitalism, not state
socialism. It was entirely different from the rugged individualism of the past, when government left every one free to
scramble for all he could get—regardless of the other fellow.
The old theory was that somehow in the battle every one
would share according to his merits. It worked fine in pioneer
days. But, in the era of great corporations, in the cosmic size
of our population and our industries, the old system broke
down. The New Dealers believed government could step in,
regulate and legislate in the public interest, could ease capitalism into a more fitting modern mold.

In Franklin D. Roosevelt's book, *Looking Forward*,
finished a few nights before he became President, he said:
"I believe that we are at the threshold of a fundamental
change in our economic thought. I believe that in the future
we are going to think less of the producer and more about
the consumer. Do what we may to inject health into our
ailing economic order, we cannot make it endure for long

unless we can bring about a wiser, more equitable distribution of the national income."

Absorbed as we were by the New Deal excitement, Ray and I read with shocked interest a letter from newspaperman Ed Beattie from Berlin. He had dined with us before he left for his assignment in Hitler's Germany. His "thank you" note told us of the real revolution being experienced as Hitler and his top men determinedly put through all their ideas. They were operating in a strange fashion and accomplishing nothing economically good for the nation. They provided pep talks and sensations. The press, he said, was practically nonexistent—every paper had been "harmonized," the slightest hint of criticism in a paper brought suspension. All government announcements were printed verbatim and without comment. Beattie ended the letter on this sinister note: "There is a lot more to be said but every one advises against putting it in the mails!"

Chapter Three

❧

IMMORTALITY
AND MEDIOCRITY
IN THE WHITE HOUSE

Iₙ 1935 MY HUSBAND ESTIMATED THAT the men of the working press in Washington were 95 percent in favor of Franklin Roosevelt as a competent man at home in his job as President of the United States. This startlingly favorable reaction was due partly to Roosevelt's own charm and ability. It was based also on the contrast he made with former men in the same job as judged by men who watched Presidents close-up.

My husband had known Presidents Harding and Coolidge personally and well. Although he came to Washington during Woodrow Wilson's second administration in 1917, while World War I was still going on, he was then a beginner in newspaper reporting. Only experienced newspapermen are assigned to cover the White House. So Ray had had no personal experience with Wilson.

Of course we talked about Wilson a lot; about his autocratic manner in telling Congress, "This is what I want, you get it through." But his democratic outlook overshadowed his methods. We were inspired by his world idealism. We picked up lots of interesting gossip about him, such as that he read the *New Republic* regularly and that to get a voice for any reform it was wise to get that magazine's support because Wilson paid so much attention to it.

The most poignant memory my husband had of Woodrow Wilson was much later—Armistice Day, 1923. Wilson had been out of the White House three years. He was a broken, ill man, living in seclusion in his S Street home. It was a raw, cloudy day. The World War had been over five years. Harding had already died in the Presidency. Coolidge was pleased with his rigid government economy program, which was bringing our expenditures within our income, and he believed we were on the threshold of a new era. The League of Nations was dead as far as the United States was concerned—people scoffed, saying it had been only the fanciful dream of an impractical college professor anyhow. It had long since ceased to be good politics to be publicly associated with the Wilson dream.

In the street outside the S Street mansion, a handful of faithful, bedraggled believers in Wilson and his dream knelt down to pray, as was their habit every Armistice Day. No one prominent was in the crowd, of course, just fringe sentimentalists, cranks, unrealistic people, misty-eyed over a broken idealist—perhaps a mother or two, mourning for war-lost sons with a grief that would never pass.

A minister said a prayer. Someone went up to the door,

knocked, and soon Wilson came out on the stoop. He dragged himself out with difficulty, leaning on a cane. Emaciated, his white hair hanging in a fringe on his neck, he seemed to pull himself together under his long black cape to make a dignified appearance. He wore his silk hat and feebly lifted it to his friends. He choked as he uttered a word of thanks. Suddenly he fired up, and speaking like an implacable prophet of the Old Testament, uttered these vibrant words:

"Just one word more. I cannot refrain from saying it: I am not one of those who have the least anxiety about the triumph of the principles I have stood for. I have seen fools resist Providence before and I have seen their destruction, as will come upon these again—utter destruction and contempt. That we shall prevail is as sure as that God reigns."

Those were the last public words that Woodrow Wilson ever spoke.

Twenty years later we were dining with Homer Cummings, Attorney General under President Franklin D. Roosevelt, who had a famous collection of autographed photographs lining the walls of his beautiful home in Washington. He pointed to an affectionately autographed photograph of Woodrow Wilson, signed just a few days after the Armistice on November 20, 1918. At that time Wilson had told him that unless the League of Nations was adopted by the United States the world was due for a long period of anarchy, in which there would be dictatorships, bloodshed, and general turmoil. Woodrow Wilson's strong feeling that

that would happen was probably responsible for his taking the defeat of the League so hard.

Homer Cummings told us how he had prepared the key-note speech for the Democratic Convention in San Francisco in 1920. President Wilson called him to the White House to go over the speech. They sat comfortably on the South Portico with Mrs. Wilson hovering close behind the invalid Wilson's chair. He had suffered two paralytic strokes. The first occurred at Pueblo, Colorado, September 26, 1919, when he was carrying his League of Nations fight to the people. His relentless, ruthless enemies, the "battalion of death," Senators Lodge, Borah, Hiram Johnson, and Reed, trailed him, conquering public support. The second stroke hit Wilson eight days after the first. He was found on the bathroom floor, having fallen while shaving. Dr. Grayson was called at once. For five or six weeks he literally was at the point of death. But after some months he improved to such an extent that specialists proclaimed him "organically sound, able-minded and able-bodied."

President Wilson himself seemed to forget how ill he had been, because after complimenting Homer Cummings on the good speech he had written he complained about a reference in it to his illness, saying, "This sentence that I was at the point of death is not true. I never was." Mrs. Wilson, standing behind his chair, shook her head at Cummings, as though to say, "Woodrow is wrong. He just doesn't know." To placate him, Mr. Cummings changed the sentence to read, "The President was very close to the point of death."

Immortality and Mediocrity in the White House

J. Fred Essary, famous writer for the Baltimore *Sun*, told us that after Wilson's second paralytic stroke Mrs. Wilson, Dr. Grayson, and Joe Tumulty, presidential secretary, felt that it would be a great mistake to make the situation public, principally because Senators Lodge and Brandegee were trying to find an excuse to put Vice President Marshall in the White House, on the grounds that the President was incapacitated so that he could not execute the duties of his office. However, the White House group felt that Marshall should be advised of the critical situation and of the real possibility that he might be called upon at any minute to take the oath of office.

Tumulty and Grayson felt that they could not so advise Marshall, that it should be done unofficially and secretly. Fred Essary was a close friend of Marshall's—they asked him to do it. He went to see the Vice President and explained the whole situation. Marshall sat at his desk—hands clasped on it—looking down at his hands. He never raised his eyes. When Fred finished talking, he waited for Marshall's response, but none came. Finally Fred rose, paused another minute, walked to the door, opened it; and, as he looked back, Marshall still sat with eyes fixed on his hands.

A couple of years later, Marshall confessed that once when in Atlanta, Georgia, during Wilson's illness, he thought he was President for one hour. He had arrived in Atlanta without fanfare to make a speech. He had a small hotel room; nobody met him or gave any parties for him. In the midst of his speech, a message was handed to him saying Wilson had died. Marshall immediately announced it to the audience, and the meeting was adjourned. Instantly body guards, a police escort, and much fanfare sprang up as if by magic to escort him back to his hotel. An hour later he was advised that the report was incorrect. He left town without a soul going to the station. He was just a plain, obscure Vice President again. Marshall said that that hour was the most agonizing of his life. He realized that he didn't want to succeed Wilson, because Wilson was so great a man that anybody following him was bound to look very small in history.

We lived only a block away from the Wilson home and used to walk over there almost daily in January, 1924. The press was keeping a death watch on the house. We'd stop to talk with the waiting reporters. One Sunday morning, February 3, 1924, we had just started up the hill toward the house when we saw reporters racing down the hill to telephone the flash that Woodrow Wilson was dead. We joined the little crowd of mourners gathered in the street before his house and stood silently thinking what this loss meant to us and to a forgetful world. My husband's words comforted me.

"Don't cry, honey. His ideas live on. They are immortal."

As we stood there, we saw a little five-year-old boy cross over to the house, ring the bell and hand a red rose to a stooped attendant. Then a young woman, poorly dressed, handed in a single white lily, the tribute of a humble soul to departed greatness.

A big black limousine rolled up. The President and Mrs. Coolidge got out and the President handed in two cards to the doorman. They turned away with solemn faces, entered their automobile and drove away.

By the time the Republican Convention met in June, 1920, Ray had spent a year writing about the activities of the House and Senate from the press galleries in the Capitol. This qualified him to go to the convention in Chicago.

Leading contenders for the Republican presidential nomination were Major General Leonard Wood and Governor Frank O. Lowden. The stalemate between them was broken by a newly created Senatorial bloc that finally agreed upon and nominated one of the Senate's own, the genial, handsome Senator Warren G. Harding, editor and publisher of the Marion, Ohio, *Star*.

The manner of making their choice has been told many times. When the leaders went into session in that famous smoke-filled room to pick a candidate, Ray kept vigil all night in the hall outside. Senator Charles Curtis of Kansas came out of the room about 3:30 A.M., found his fellow Kansan still hanging about and tipped him off that it looked like Harding. This gave Ray his first big scoop and priority on the assignment of covering Harding during his campaign for the Presidency.

I remember a story about that smoke-filled room. When the men had decided upon Harding as the candidate, some one brought up the gossip about Harding's love life. This gossip had appeared in every previous political campaign that Harding had waged for governorship and Senate. There was also the accusation, a typically unfounded campaign smear story, that one of Harding's forebears had Negro blood. One cautious participant suggested Harding be brought into the room and questioned. Harding came in and was asked, "Is there anything on your conscience that would prevent you from accepting the Republican nomination for the Presidency?"

Harding begged for a few moments to think it over. He was shown to the only private spot, the coat closet in the room. A few minutes later he emerged, smoothed his rumpled shock of iron-gray hair and said, "Gentlemen, I have consulted my God and can say to you that there is nothing to prevent me from accepting the nomination of our great party."

It was a cheerful campaign waged from the front porch of the rambling brick house in Marion, Ohio. Although the country had Prohibition and Harding himself was scrupulous about serving alcohol, his friends were less careful. Newspapermen lived and drank well. Harding considered himself a newspaperman and included newspaper people in festivities more than is usual. The Republican National Committee provided a fine Lincoln limousine for the newsmen, and we followed the candidate everywhere—to his golf club, to his picnics with Henry Ford and Harvey Firestone.

I joined my husband in Marion, Ohio, twice during the campaign. I met candidate and Mrs. Harding; handsome

George Christian, Harding's secretary; Jimmie Sloan, Harding's personal secret service man; Judson Welliver, witty and puckish speechwriter for the candidate, and hundreds of men and women connected with that successful campaign.

Mrs. Byron Price, wife of the young, enterprising reporter for the Associated Press, who in World War II did such a skillful job as United States censor, was my companion and friend on occasional campaign train trips we were allowed to take. Once the train stopped in Dayton for the candidate to make a rear-end train speech to the assembled multitude. Priscilla Price, Judson Welliver, Sam Williamson, reporter for the New York *Times*, and I got off the train to stretch our legs. We walked back to the rear of the train to hear Harding's speech. Suddenly the train began to move. We raced beside the train, trying to reach our Pullman. We got there in time for Sam to throw Priscilla aboard, but the porter with his little white step, Judd, Sam and I were left on the platform. I had no coat, hat or purse.

As the train whisked out of sight, I had a fleeting glimpse of my husband's astonished face behind Senator Harding's waving arm. Harding saw us, yanked the bell cord to stop the train, but to no avail. We were left behind. Embarrassed, chagrined, we climbed aboard the next train out. Judd and Sam, though hatless, fortunately had money in their pockets. We caught up with the party at the next stop, where Harding was speaking for an hour, not from his train but in an auditorium.

Ray was very angry. He felt I had no right to be aboard

anyhow; to cause all that commotion was unforgiveable. Byron was mad at Priscilla, too, even though she made the train. Our sin was to have called spectacular attention to our presence. Our husbands thought Harding might be angry, that they might be reprimanded and withdrawn from their assignments. They locked us in our staterooms and wouldn't speak to us for hours.

Frequently attached to the Harding special train was a luxurious private car belonging to Mr. and Mrs. Edward B. McLean. He was the wealthy publisher of the Washington *Post* and the Cincinnati *Inquirer*. She was the daughter of Tom Walsh, who discovered the famous Camp Bird Gold Mine at Ouray, Colorado, one of the richest gold strikes in history. We used to watch Mrs. McLean with fascination as she paced a station platform, attended always by a private detective, the Hope Diamond around her neck, diamond hatpins in her hat and a half dozen priceless bracelets on her arm.

In her plain blue print dresses, Mrs. Harding seemed quite a contrast to Mrs. McLean. "The Duchess," as everyone called Mrs. Harding, had a dominant personality, seeking expression in the restricted opportunities offered to the wife of a public man in those days when Presidents' wives were supposed to be seen, not heard. Florence Kling Harding was a sharp judge of human nature and probably would have made a better President than her husband. She had a sense of foreboding throughout his campaign and once told Ray she imagined she saw "tragedy" written over her husband's head.

On election night, we gathered at the press shack in the yard to get the telegraphic reports. By 10 P.M. the result was certain. Harding won by a landslide. James Cox was defeated, along with his vice-presidential running mate, Franklin D. Roosevelt. Harding sent two bottles of champagne to us to celebrate—only two bottles for at least twenty people. Other contributions came in, however, and we celebrated most of the night. I remember we chose Priscilla as chairman of the hilarity. The men lifted her up onto a table, where she stood like a doll while we danced about her singing and laughing.

Harding was sworn in, March 4, 1921—a cold but sunny day. While Ray hovered close to him to report every phase of the ceremony, I watched and listened, standing among the milling thousands in the streets around the Capitol. It was my first inauguration. The address seemed uninspired and rather dull.

I think all of us were unconscious of the amount of gossip and intrigue about the President-Elect that burst into national scandal later. We did hear about the Marion lady who had been sent off to China with her obliging husband, so that during the campaign no tongues could wag; but we knew nothing of Nan Britton, author of *The President's Daughter*.

Long after Harding's death, my husband was told by a friend of President Harding's the remarkable story of the night before his inauguration. The President-Elect and Mrs.

Harding were occupying the presidential suite at the Willard Hotel. Harding's friends were worried about the arrival that night at the hotel of one of his lady friends. They didn't want any scandal on the eve of his inauguration. They cautioned Harding to stay in his room. But apparently they didn't trust him where a pretty woman was concerned, for they kept a vigil out in the hall all night. Sure enough, before the night was over, the President-Elect tiptoed out into the hall. His friends pushed him back into the room. Then they went upstairs, knocked on the lady's door, and ordered her to pack and get out of town, threatening to put the F.B.I. on her trail if she didn't go at once. She was so frightened she left immediately.

Ray's new assignment was to cover the White House. His close association with the new President made this logical. Our living room now sported autographed photographs of the President and the First Lady.

Soon after the Hardings were settled in the White House, Mrs. Harding told Ray she would like to have me call upon her. I didn't know exactly how to do this, but I had read that many people were leaving calling cards at the White House. So one day I drove our Model T Ford, which we had extravagantly purchased a few months before, up to the Pennsylvania Avenue entrance. I was worried and frightened for fear I wouldn't do the correct thing. Should I have parked the car and walked up? Should I leave the Ford forlornly sitting under the portico, walk up and ring the doorbell?

I need not have worried, because as the car came to a stop, a fine Negro doorman, in formal dress, came down the steps to the car and held out a silver card tray. I fumbled for my cards. I needed two for my husband and one for myself. A husband, technically, calls on the President and the First Lady, while his wife calls only on the First Lady. Gingerly I dropped three cards onto the tray. With a nod and a superior air of finality, the servitor moved majestically away. I drove off, relieved.

A few days later I received a little note from Mrs. Harding, "Please come in for a cup of tea on Monday at five." This time I parked the car and walked boldly up. The same august doorman surprised me by his greeting, "Mrs. Clapper, this way, please," and I walked behind him through the hall and upstairs where Mrs. Harding received me in the family living room. I pinched myself because at last I was actually a guest in the White House.

Inside, the White House seems a coldly austere establishment with vast marble rooms and halls carpeted with hundreds of yards of red carpet. Many Presidents' wives have struggled in vain to make it look homelike by moving furniture about, adding new decorations and all manner of draperies. The first floor, the only part of the mansion that sightseers ever see, consists of the East Room, the Green Room, the Blue Room, the Red Room, the State Dining Room, the Breakfast Room and vast hallways that cover more square feet than the rooms themselves.

But the oval-shaped sitting room on the second floor has

cheerful comfort as the sun streams through its circular windows. Here are warm-toned rugs, books, sofas, easy chairs. It is like any comfortable living room. The second floor has seven large bedrooms. When, later, the Calvin Coolidges moved in, the attic on the third floor was converted into thirteen small bedrooms, and the White House boasted fourteen bathrooms.

To me that day, Mrs. Harding seemed quite changed. She had a beautiful wardrobe of new clothes from New York and almost seemed suited for the role of First Lady. She moved with dignity, in place of the gawkiness I remembered in Marion, Ohio. There she had usually worn blue print dresses with high collars, or a ribbon dog collar. She clung to high-buttoned shoes long after every one else was wearing low-cut pumps. This day, her dress was a soft gray with beautiful lace billowing down her gaunt figure. Gray pumps matched her dress. Her iron-gray hair looked softer too, not primly set in hard waves as it had been.

Of course there were other guests, and I was too shy to try to talk. I sat uncomfortably drinking hot tea, and left in exactly fifteen minutes, because someone had told me that was the correct thing to do.

Less than a month after his inauguration, Harding invited the twelve newspapermen who had been with him during his campaign to dinner. They called themselves "The Elephant Club." This club was similar to the famous "cuff-link" club of Franklin Roosevelt, who included in his "club" those men who had been associated with him in his 1920 campaign and to whom he gave identical sets of cuff links. The Elephant Club expired with Harding.

This dinner was Ray's first in the State Dining Room of the Executive Mansion. Harding started off the dinner by telling the newspapermen the conversation he had with President Woodrow Wilson as they rode up Pennsylvania Avenue to the Capitol for Harding's inauguration ceremonies. The newspapermen knew that Harding had shown gentle consideration for his stricken predecessor and had actually helped lift Wilson down the White House steps into their carriage. As they moved off toward the Capitol where Harding would take the oath of office there was at first an embarrassed silence between the two men. Then Harding began to talk about White House pets. That led to a talk of pets in general, and Harding told Wilson about his sister, a missionary in India who had been touched by the story of the devotion of a dying elephant. The animal moaned piteously for his keeper in his last hours. The keeper was summoned. Folding the man to him tenderly with his trunk, the animal peacefully passed away. As Harding concluded the story, to his astonishment, he saw tears coursing down Wilson's face.

After dinner that night, Mr. Harding took his guests upstairs to his study. They saw his dressing room and the old, extra-sized bed that Lincoln and Wilson slept on. Harding's golf suit, worn that day, was on a rack; golf balls, neckties and carpet slippers were strewn about. The study walls were lined with books. Harding showed them the "yellow book" of press clippings made up for him each day. He called it his bedfellow for every night. He read political and financial news hastily, editorials carefully. To me afterward, Ray remarked it was like spending a pleasant evening with the editor of the Marion *Star* instead of the President of the United States. "It was strangely impressive," he added, "because of its simplicity."

Harding had hedged a lot during his campaign about his views of the United States joining the League of Nations. He aroused public opinion again and again against the League by calling it a "super-government of the world" and said that he wanted "America to continue to determine her own way and not permit a council of foreign powers around a table in Geneva to say what we shall do to play our part in the world." But he also spoke of a possible "Association of Nations," as he called it, to be substituted for the League.

His stand became clear when he sent his first message to the extraordinary session of Congress on April 12, 1921, flatly stating that the United States would not accept membership in the League. Incidentally, it is interesting to note that technically we were still at war with Germany, because the Senate would not ratify the Treaty of Versailles. Not until July, 1921, did Harding sign a joint Congressional resolution declaring peace with Germany and Austria.

Ray went everywhere the President went. One trip lingered in his memory. On May 23, 1921, they attended brief services at an army pier in Hoboken for 6,000 war dead whose bodies had just arrived from France. The President and Mrs. Harding walked through the pale gray haze

among the flag-draped pine boxes. The President mounted
a rude platform. A muffled band played the solemn strains
of Chopin's funeral march. After a prayer, the President
rose, struggling with strong emotion, as his eye reached the
relatives gathered for the service. Tears in his eyes, words
came brokenly: "A hundred thousand sorrows are touching
my heart." Pointing to the coffins, "God grant this may not
be again."

A newspaperman, writing of the doings of a President,
sees and records the sad, the happy, the absurd, and the sub-
lime eddies of life around that man. In a single day, Herbert
Hoover, General John J. Pershing, and Samuel Gompers
called at the White House, along with that old hermit of
journalism, E. W. Scripps, who controlled his chain of newspapers from the mysterious recesses of his secluded estate at
San Diego, California.

Booth Tarkington came in with Mary Roberts Rinehart,
who vowed she wanted the people to hear every word about
the armament conference and would hide in a coal scuttle
if necessary to get the facts before the people.

Sir Harry Lauder came to breakfast, ready to play golf
afterward, wearing his kilts. Another day, Sergeant Samuel
Woodfill, who had been described at one time by General
Pershing as the greatest private in the World War, was
brought to shake hands. Will Rogers too was presented, and
Harding said, "This is the first time I ever got to see you
without paying for it."

The year 1921 had its somber note. Etched in memory

with deep emotional feelings was the burial of the unknown soldier of the World War. He had been picked by a special committee from the thousands killed in France. None knew who he was or from whence he had come. He was only an American soldier who died "to make the world safe for democracy." Now he was to be buried at Arlington with full military honors and his shrine to be guarded forever by marching sentries in front of the Arlington Amphitheater.

The day was cold but shimmeringly clear. I stood on the street in front of the White House. As the funeral entourage turned into Pennsylvania Avenue, I saw its leaders, the silver-haired President of the United States and the equally silver-haired General of the Armies, John J. Pershing. If ever two men in the prime of life looked their parts, these two magnificent figures did on that day. They were of equal height and marched side by side, erect, handsome, solemn.

Next came the flag-draped casket on a horse-drawn caisson. As it passed, every eye was wet. The war came back to us as that mute evidence of mankind's inhumanity to man moved slowly before us.

Muffled bands played funeral marches, soldiers and armament wheeled past. But the moment fraught with greatest feeling for me, at least, was when an open carriage, a square landau drawn by two horses, came at the end of the procession. It was driven by a Negro coachman. Seated inside were two figures, the still beautiful Edith Bolling Wilson and the crumpled, ailing figure of Woodrow Wilson. His days of glory were over. The gallant fight he had made for morality among nations awaited another generation for vindication.

Ray did not accompany President Harding on his fatal trip to Alaska. He telephoned me from his office about eight o'clock, the night of August 2, 1923, and in a grief-choked voice, said, "Harding died in San Francisco, half an hour ago. He was struck with cerebral apoplexy, and he passed away. I have lost a good friend."

Throughout the next five years the world learned of the proved crimes or undisputed facts that made Harding's memory almost a rag in the gutter: Albert B. Fall, Secretary of the Interior, convicted of accepting a bribe and sentenced to jail; Charles R. Forbes, head of the Veterans' Bureau, convicted of defrauding the government and sent to jail; Thomas W. Miller, Alien Property Custodian, convicted of accepting money to influence an official action and sent to jail; Harry M. Daugherty, Attorney General, indicted for faithlessness to duty; Jess Smith, Harding's intimate, a suicide after he had accepted more than fifty thousand dollars to facilitate a case before the Alien Property Custodian.

The curious thing about President Harding was that every one loved him in spite of this horrible debacle of his administration. We blamed his friends who betrayed him and felt much as Herbert Hoover did when he dedicated a memorial to President Harding in Marion:

"We came to know that there was a man whose soul was being seared by a great disillusionment. We saw him grad-

· 67 ·

ually weaken, not only from physical exhaustion but from mental anxiety. Warren Harding had a dim realization that he had been betrayed by a few of the men he had trusted, by men he had believed were his devoted friends. It was later proved in the courts of the land that these men had betrayed not alone the friendship and trust of their staunch and loyal friend but they had betrayed their country. That was the tragedy of the life of Warren Harding."

Chapter Four

NEW ENGLAND
CONTRIBUTES THE
MAN OF THE HOUR

C ALVIN COOLIDGE WAS NEVER AGAIN AS appealing and human as he was the night of August 2, 1923, when he was awakened in his father's farmhouse at Plymouth, Vermont. He had gone peacefully to sleep that night on the assurance of a long distance talk with President Harding's physicians that the President was on the road to recovery.

Coolidge himself told of his thoughts that night— thoughts of the sacrifices his father had made to help him to rise to a position of authority, of twenty-five-mile drives in blizzards over mountain roads to carry Calvin to the academy, of all the tender care lavished on a motherless boy. He visited his mother's grave that night, too, because it was his habit to go there whenever he was troubled.

He seemed to bring a stern but calm Yankee atmosphere to the White House. Although the Coolidge administration rocked with Congressional investigations and criminal trials born of misdeeds of the Harding regime, it was otherwise placid because the country prospered. No international crisis occurred to jar us from our complacent isolation, and the government at Washington minded its own business, allowing every one to make all the money his native ability permitted.

President Calvin Coolidge arose daily at 6:30 A.M. for a twenty-minute, prebreakfast walk, not through the natural beauty spots of Washington, but through the business streets where milk wagons trundled along and a few sleepy streetcars began their regular runs. He would be dressed in a carefully pressed double-breasted business suit, a high stiff-collared shirt, and a muffler if the morning was raw.

After a frugal breakfast—fruit, cereal and coffee—the President looked over newspaper headlines, then his list of the day's appointments. Lunch came at one o'clock, after he had received visitors of all sorts. In the afternoon he answered mail, signed papers. By 6:30 P.M. his desk was clear and in perfect order. After dinner at seven, he went to his study to read some nonfiction book. Coolidge almost never went to the theater, and no movies were shown at the White House then. At 9:45 P.M. he was in bed.

He seldom traveled, yet Washington seemed to impress him very little. His rock-bound New England habits remained. On warm summer nights his predecessors had enjoyed sitting in splendor on the south portico of the White House. Cal's favorite pastime was to sit in a straight-backed rocker on the small north porch so that he could intently watch the streetcars go past the White House.

When an old lady clerk, carrying his first pay check to Coolidge, made a speech about all the Presidents from McKinley to Coolidge to whom she had carried pay checks, Cal listened quietly. When she was through, he simply said, "Come again."

Coolidge always managed quietly to get revenge on any one whom he disliked. One particular instance had to do with the French Ambassador, Jusserand. He had served in this country for many years with a notable record. But unfortunately, shortly before he was to retire, he was invited to address a ladies' literary club in Washington. That was along about 1926 or so. The war debts were a touchy subject; and Ambassador Jusserand, voicing what was being said all over Europe, told the ladies about the great sacrifices France had made and how she ought not to be compelled to pay blood money in the form of war debts. Accounts of this speech happened to be printed just before one of President Coolidge's press conferences. A question was asked about it.

Coolidge's lips tightened, and he said: "If the French Ambassador has any proposals to make about the war debts, he should present them to the State Department."

This was a severe rebuke, and Ambassador Jusserand, just rounding out a long and successful career, was of course greatly upset. He appealed to the State Department to get him out from under the cloud of the presidential rebuke. The pressure was so strong that shortly thereafter President

Coolidge was persuaded to issue a formal statement denying he had rebuked the French Ambassador.

Before long came the White House diplomatic reception, and a slight mishap gave Coolidge his revenge. Jusserand was dean of the diplomatic corps and therefore custom required that he lead the procession of diplomats into the Blue Room to be received by the President. This function calls for the full regimentals of the diplomatic protocol—those gorgeous gold-braided, highly uncomfortable uniforms which the diplomats reluctantly climb into when custom requires. They are a good deal like most men's dress suits—something held over from college days and worn as long as the steadily enlarging girth of middle age will permit vest and trousers to meet in happy union.

Jusserand's waistcoat was tight, and his custom was to lay it beside him in his automobile and put it on in the dressing room at the White House. On this particular night, he got out of his car and forgot it. His car drove off, the chauffeur with orders to return at 10:30 P.M. Inside the White House, Jusserand realized his predicament. One of his aides telephoned the Embassy frantically. The chauffeur was not coming back there, they said. He was going to see his girl, named Magnolia. She lived at an unknown address in the vicinity of U Street and Florida Avenue. The White House police were called into consultation, and they obtained a squad of metropolitan motorcycle police and started at top speed for Magnolia's neighborhood to find the embassy car. Meantime, word was sent up to President Coolidge of the situation, and it was suggested that he might delay the reception a short time until the waistcoat was recovered.

This was Coolidge's moment. Without batting an eyelash, he ordered the reception to begin at the scheduled moment. The Marine Band in its scarlet tunics struck up *Hail to the Chief*. The President and Mrs. Coolidge came down the grand staircase and took their places in the Blue Room. The diplomats filed by and Ambassador Jusserand paced the floor downstairs. Eventually there was a shrieking of motor-cycle sirens outside, a hurried dash by two men into the cloak room, and Ambassador Jusserand was hustled into his waistcoat and upstairs to the Blue Room. The line was almost through. He fell in at the end, and forcing a smile as only a veteran diplomat could under the circumstances, bowed as he shook the presidential hand. As quickly as he could, he departed—feeling no doubt much as Magnolia did —that the evening had not been a decided social success.

The habitual taciturnity that gave Coolidge the nickname "Silent Cal" is best illustrated by an episode told to me by the Chief Justice of the Supreme Court, Harlan Fiske Stone. The first time he met Coolidge was at breakfast one morning at the Adams House in Boston. Stone was breakfasting with his own father, who had had some business interest which Coolidge's law firm had handled. Coolidge was then Governor of Massachusetts. He saw the Stones, greeted them, sat down at their table. With not another word Coolidge ate, then rose, said good-bye, and left.

Stone Junior remarked to his father, "You would think

he didn't want to see us. But he voluntarily came over and sat down, so he must have wanted to see us!"

After Coolidge became President, Harlan Fiske Stone in New York received a telephone call from Coolidge in Washington. . . . "Doing anything tonight?" . . . "Nothing except going to a concert." . . . "Catch a midnight train and come straight to the White House."

Stone arrived in time for breakfast. Coolidge had several Senators in. Then Cal went to his office. When lunch came, Cal still explained nothing. Late that day, Cal asked Stone to suggest some names to handle the oil prosecutions. Stone suggested Owen J. Roberts, later Supreme Court Justice— then a young lawyer in Philadelphia. Cal had never heard of him, but looked him up and took him. Then they talked a bit about the Attorney General, Harry Daugherty. He was in the very hot water of the Harding administration scandals. Finally Coolidge said, "I want you to take it." Although Stone demurred, he finally accepted the Cabinet post.

Later that day, Representative Snell called and urged Coolidge to appoint Stone. Cal let him talk on and didn't tell him it was already done. To Snell's amazement, as he walked out of the White House, newspaper reporters told him Stone's nomination had just gone to the Senate!

Justice Stone recalled that Coolidge would always see him on Justice Department business, but his instructions were: "Remember the United States Government is your client. You make the decisions."

Another time, a caller was asked by Coolidge if he knew

Jim Beck, then Solicitor General. "A very interesting situation, there," Coolidge said, as the caller waited expectantly. "He wants to go to London as ambassador. He spent half an hour telling me considerations that should win the appointment." His caller said, "I'm sure you were aware of the many considerations in his favor before." Cal said, "Yes. Less now."

On one hot summer day, Coolidge took a group of newspapermen on the Presidential yacht for a cool trip down the Potomac. Most of the time he stood on the deck against the rail, gazing at the Virginia farms on the beautiful shoreline. One by one, a secretary routed the men to his side for a talk. Comparing notes later, the newspapermen discovered that all he said to any of them was, "That's a pretty white or red house or barn over there," depending on the structure they happened to be passing.

He had a streak of the practical joker in him, delighting to make secret service men wear rubbers over their shoes and carry umbrellas on the sunniest days. Sometimes it amounted almost to sadism, though perhaps quite unintentionally so. His secret service companions told Ray that Coolidge would ask them to bait his fishhook on fishing trips. At the moment when the worm was almost on the hook, as the agent held the deadly pointed hook between his fingers, Coolidge would impatiently yank the line, snagging the man's finger and drawing blood.

Calvin Coolidge, having served a term and a half as President, issued a preconvention statement that he did not "choose" to run for President in 1928. The argument over his intention and meaning consumed reams of newspaper lineage, but the Republican Convention chose to take Coolidge's meaning literally and nominated Herbert Hoover for the highest office. Judson Welliver, secretary to both President Harding and President Coolidge, told Ray that he knew positively that Coolidge thought his "choose" statement was the best way to be renominated. When William Butler, Chairman of the Republican National Committee, gave out his statement that "this took Coolidge out of the race," Coolidge sent him a scorching telegram. Later, Coolidge went to great lengths over a period of weeks, to get back every copy of the telegram.

Justice Harlan Fiske Stone called on President Coolidge on his last day in the White House. Cal was lonesome, as all Presidents are on that day. Stone said, "I'm glad you are leaving, because the next four years are going to see the worst financial debacle since 1873." Coolidge answered, "It is always better to go while they still want you," not sensing, apparently, what was coming.

One day in November, 1931, my husband asked me to go up to the exquisite new Folger Shakespearean Library on Capitol Hill and find out if they had Queen Elizabeth's corsets there. Ex-President Calvin Coolidge had asked Ray to find out, but Ray felt too shy to ask—so he made me do it. I went. "Yes," they told me, "her corsets are here, but they are so old and fragile we have to keep them from public display in order to preserve them."

This errand came about as a result of a visit Ray paid to Coolidge in Northampton. He found the former President mellow and very chatty. They sat in rocking chairs on the front porch, feet up on the porch rail, and talked for hours.

The first thing Coolidge said was, "I hear the Folger Shakespearean Library is finished and open to the public. Wish I could see it. Hear they got Queen Elizabeth's corsets there. Understand there was quite a tussle in London between rich collectors to get them when they were put up for sale. Folger must have paid a lot for them. Like to see 'em. Let me know if they really have them there, will you?"

He chuckled and proceeded to answer some of Ray's questions.

In answer to one of them he said, "No, I won't do any writing. It might look as though I were trying to run the country. I don't have access to information here. I thought I might travel, but, if I travel, it requires speeches, and there is the danger of saying something that would cause the new administration embarrassment. While I was President, I would not have wanted an ex-President poking around Europe. Volunteer diplomats are bad enough, but an ex-President is too important abroad. No, I can't write or travel either. I seem to be always in the way now."

When Ray complimented him on his good health, Coolidge said, "I feel fine, but I'm all burned out."

They talked long about the depression. Coolidge felt that every one wanted the government to go into the other fellow's business but stay out of his own. He laughed as he recalled how, when he was President, a delegation from the Chamber of Commerce would come in bearing in one hand a petition to reduce taxes and, in the other, recommendations for large projects which would cost plenty of taxpayers' money. In dealing with Congress, he found it was better not to say what he wanted because some members would immediately decide to vote against it; whereas, if he kept still, he would get some of those votes. Coolidge had a rule: when he did a thing he never gave a reason for doing it. He said, "Let every one supply his own reason." Thus he felt he pleased not only those who might have agreed with his reason but also those who might approve his action but not his reason for it.

When Ray told me all that Coolidge had said, he chuckled, because Coolidge never referred to President Hoover by name but always as "that man." Coolidge just didn't like Hoover, but he wouldn't do anything to embarrass or handicap him.

Coolidge died suddenly, fourteen months later. Some one wisecracked that "something awful must be about to happen to the country, because Cal always got out just in time."

Chapter Five

A COSTLY LESSON
TO BE REMEMBERED

M Y HUSBAND OFTEN SAID, "GREATNESS
is partly in the man, partly in the times." Each of the four
sincere men who preceded Franklin D. Roosevelt as President of the United States had tried to meet the requirements
of his time. But occasionally some of our greatest men are
whipped by the times. Roosevelt himself came close to being
whipped by the stubborn unemployment problems and the
hatred he aroused in the big business group.

His predecessors had had to meet crises of one kind or
another. Roosevelt faced not only unemployment of twelve
millions, bank failures, and an economic order that had outgrown its political framework, but also a nation paralyzed by
panic.

The mystery of current American politics was the fear so
many business men had of Roosevelt. They never tumbled
to the fact that he was a mild man. The real gun at their
backs was held in the hands of the unemployed—the ill-
housed, ill-clothed, and ill-fed suffering millions, who
listened to the Huey Longs, the Townsends and the Cough-

lins. It was these men who fed the sufferers bitter medicine; Roosevelt, at most, used milk of magnesia. Emil Ludwig sized it up when he said in his biography of Roosevelt: "The sons of those Americans who are opposing Roosevelt today will perhaps some day erect a monument to him as the last of those who fought to preserve their system."

Roosevelt's bark was worse than his bite. As an English journalist put it, American conservatives were busy describing a roving domestic cat as a raging Bengal tiger.

Ray traveled from coast to coast in 1934; he returned to Washington tired and dusty, observing that in spite of drought, depression, racketeers, chinch bugs and the New Deal, the country was going to survive. He said, "There are still a surprising number of people who insist on trying to make a living and having a decent amount of fun doing it." He found green pastures, sleek herds, bulging apple orchards, vineyards drooping with purple grapes, and people going to see Shirley Temple. But for every acre of good tidings there was another of tragedy. We still had displaced farmers, "grapes of wrath," and ten million unemployed who wanted jobs.

Our continued unemployment problem vexed everyone. A facetious newspaperman, impressed with the new frozen food, suggested that maybe the solution was to put the unemployed in cold storage, label them as to crafts, haul them out and thaw them when needed. That way, they would require no food or clothing in the meantime.

While there were more millionaires than ever, there were

also as many people unemployed as in 1932; many more sharecroppers left their dusty farms to wander in a tide of displaced people. We just didn't know how to cut the economic cloth to fit the new situation. One trouble was that many people didn't recognize that the situation had changed. Instead of buckling down to adjustments, they frustrated themselves with nostalgia for the past.

I know one successful lawyer, Joseph Davies, and one very wealthy woman, Mrs. Marjorie Post Hutton, whose romance stemmed from their mutual appreciation of what Franklin Roosevelt was trying to do; who realized that he was "concerned not so much that the rich should sleep peacefully in their beds as that everyone should have a bed in which to sleep."

It happened in Florida where Joseph Davies had gone for a month's vacation one winter. He visited several millionaire friends in their winter palaces, went fishing on their yachts and golfed on their private golf links. Toward the end of his stay he was included in a dinner party which Mrs. Hutton, the divorced wife of E. F. Hutton, gave. As Davies gazed around the table he saw that every man present was a millionaire who had been wealthy before Roosevelt came to the Presidency. Each one was wealthier now. He listened, as he had been listening for a month, to their snide remarks about the President. He pondered the dreary repetition of their fears that Roosevelt was trying to overthrow our democratic form of government. All too well Davies knew that these fears were prompted by selfish desires to be allowed to pile up more and more money and power for themselves, rather than by any concern for their country.

Suddenly he could no longer stand the insults he heard about the President. After a farewell toast had been drunk to Mr. Davies because he was leaving the winter paradise to go back to work, he rose and proposed a toast to the President of the United States. Consternation ricocheted across the table. In calm tones he explained that daily they had inflicted upon his ears their insults to his Commander in Chief and friend. Now it was his turn to answer back. He pointed his finger at each man individually as he calculated that man's worldly wealth in 1932 and the increase in each case after Roosevelt came into office. He pointed out that had Roosevelt not prevented hunger for millions of men, women, and children, had he not been the symbol of hope to millions of the unemployed, there would have been revolution and bloodshed. "Where would your millions be if that had happened?" asked Joe Davies.

For twenty minutes he held the floor. He sat down amid shocked silence. Then the exquisitely beautiful hostess, Marjorie Hutton, clapped her hands, rose from her seat, walked around the table to Mr. Davies and kissed him. And so it is said their romance began.

Roosevelt appointed Davies Ambassador to the Soviet Union and later Ambassador to Belgium. Davies served Roosevelt well as a diplomat in Europe before the war, and in Russia he was honored as an honest capitalist who made no bones about his beliefs.

A Costly Lesson To Be Remembered

The general public seemed very much uninterested in foreign affairs in the middle thirties. Ray and I had sat through the Disarmament Conference during the Harding administration. We had hailed the Kellogg-Briand Peace Pact as proof of the good intentions of the nations to outlaw war.

And Ray had gone to the five-power naval conference in London in 1930. That conference of Great Britain, the United States, France, Japan, and Italy was the third attempt within a decade to reduce the heavy burdens of naval competition in the world. These nations were operating on the theory that if we had less toys lying around with which to play we wouldn't be so apt to play.

The naval conference failed to make any notable progress toward either naval disarmament or world peace, but it gave Ray his first foreign experience under glittering circumstances. He soon adjusted to the ways of London—even its strange lefthand traffic. Like others with the delegation, he felt he could get around town all right "if the English would just speak English."

Ray was struck by the universal courtesy of Englishmen, whether Members of Parliament or taxi drivers. But, in spite of the more leisurely living in England, like many Americans in London for the first time, he felt that he preferred the bouncing zest of American life. He was amazed at what the British, reaching out from their little island, had accomplished in building a great world empire.

He sensed that the British realized from the moment World War I ended that they would be hopelessly outclassed by the United States, much like an aging baseball pitcher whose steam is pretty well gone, but who holds on by his wits, long experience, superior judgment, while the youngster depends on his native strength—and the outcome is only a matter of time.

Ray didn't like the bitter, penetrating weather of England. He was cold at Nancy Astor's, cold at Chequers—where the Prime Minister entertained the visiting newspapermen and nearly froze them to death on a long hike; he was cold at banquets at the French Embassy; at Whitehall; at Londonderry House, "to meet the Duke and Duchess of York"; at the Queen's Theatre, where he saw Bernard Shaw's "The Apple Cart"; and at Stoke Poges Church.

He warmed up only when, with Charlie Ross, of the St. Louis *Post Dispatch*, he uncovered an unsavory attempt on the part of some of the United States delegation at a secret proposal to build a new thirty-three-thousand-ton battleship. Always alive to public sentiment, the newsmen knew this was contrary to the whole spirit of the disarmament conference. Sanguinely, American public opinion believed at that time that equal reduction of naval armament among nations would prevent awful wars. When the newspapermen blasted loose the secret battleship proposal, they were only spearheading the fear we had at that time of our big Navy men and big shipbuilders.

The conference became a tug of war that lasted many weeks. Each nation tried to get by with the least scrapping of the particular kind of naval craft in which it had put its faith—submarines, destroyers, battleships. Not much thought was given to that tremendously powerful naval vessel of the Second World War—the aircraft carrier.

But the most glaring omission of the conference was that two of the most powerful nations of the world were not invited to participate—Germany and the Soviet Union. It made little difference for the future whether France and Italy disagreed about destroyers and submarines, but it made a whale of a difference what Germany and Russia were doing! As Karl Bickel, astute manager of the United Press, said, "By 1950 no one will care whether France or Italy go to war or not, because their influence will be so localized. Our diplomats ought to be looking twenty years ahead, when the picture will be very different."

The conference ended with little accomplished. The correspondents came home convinced that the United States was a paradise compared to depressing Europe. Ray was pretty sick of the spectacle of a group of governments, flourishing the Kellogg-Briand Peace Pact in one hand and with the other reaching for as many 8-inch guns as they could gather; refusing to agree among themselves, while Germany blithely continued to rearm.

For the most part none of us cared much. It never occurred to us that the airplane and other modern inventions were shrinking the world, that economic and political stresses in one place could throw everything out of joint in another, and that in a flash of time a world revolution would have all nations by the throat.

Chapter Six

SHINING KNIGHTS
OF THE NEW ORDER

WITH ARMOR OF SHINING IDEALISM, the New Dealers, spearheaded by the braintrusters, moved into Washington, shouting in effect, "We shall make America over." They were an indefatigable group who worked all hours of the day and night. For the most part young men, they approached every problem as clever college professors. They argued, conferred, maneuvered, with the greatest enthusiasm. To have a chance to put some of their ideas into practice was the realization of a dream that has haunted students for years.

They were ridiculed unmercifully, but they brought a much-needed new approach to government—technical, competent men, interested in good administration for its own sake. Because few of them had official Congressional backing, drawing their power from the executive, they were seriously handicapped. It is not effusive to say that they truly understood the complexities of modern government which will never be able to function properly unless such technicians are officially attached.

Shining Knights of the New Order

A newcomer who fascinated me particularly was a woman holding high public office, Frances Perkins, Secretary of Labor. I wondered what it must be like as a woman to represent the workers of the United States at the Cabinet table. She was a tenacious official and never went home crying that she would resign if they didn't treat her well.

She turned out to be no radical. Her program always was that of the old-fashioned, 19th-century liberal: abolishment of child labor and sweat shops, more pay and comfort for the workers, more social security and unemployment insurance. She managed to juggle Bill Green and John L. Lewis fairly well, keeping them both mollified, but she said that John L. Lewis was the only one "Mama can't spank." She saved President Roosevelt the dilemma of choosing between an A.F.L. or a C.I.O. man for the Labor Cabinet post, by the simple expedient of staying there herself. She was certainly as stable as any man would have been in the post during such a difficult period.

Some people said she was arrogant. She did have a brusqueness of speech and seemed to fear no one. In the beginning she did many undiplomatic things. . . . She kept Senators waiting. Her press relations were bad, until a correspondent told her that the press could help her if she'd change her attitude. She did.

Her dinners were delightful, and the conversations anything but dull. She was no social butterfly, but she did love parties. I'll never forget one cocktail party honoring the actor Melvyn Douglas, at which Miss Perkins was ranking guest. None of us could correctly leave before her, but as she was charmed by the gallant Melvyn she stayed hours, causing some of us to miss dinner engagements.

Caroline O'Day, a friend of mine who shared Miss Perkins' house for a time, told me that Frances Perkins did not enjoy music. If she had to listen, she worked out a mathematical formula of the music. For relaxation, Miss Perkins read Greek!

The Cabinet member who interested me most as I came to know him, and whose career may have the greatest impact in the next ten years on our nation, was Henry Wallace —simple and humble outwardly, complex inwardly. None of the usual delineations fit him, probably because he fits no usual mold or type. You cannot describe him in the usual words, because he is not motivated by the usual political standards. Often you can say a man does this or that because he wants a certain office. You can't say that of Wallace. He is not so much unselfish as he is selfless. It baffles every one. He is hard to talk to, never glib; and he makes people self-conscious as they search for small talk to bridge embarrassing silences.

He looks like a farmer—you can almost see the corn tassels sticking out of his hair. Never giving a sense of bustle or speed, he literally runs wherever he goes. He is always in perfect physical condition, with the energy and strength of a trained athlete. He is perpetually young in his activities and in his ability to learn new things of all kinds—from a new language to flying an airplane; from the study of hog-corn ratios to knowledge of the solar system. If he seems vague and philosophical at times, don't be deceived. He is a fighter with a bulldog grip.

For instance, there was the time back in 1934 when he split with George Peek, Administrator of the AAA. They disagreed over crop reduction. Wallace was personally fond of Peek. In the fight that developed it was Peek who went under, not Wallace. They sat side by side at a press conference in Wallace's office. Without an unkind word, Wallace calmly, forcefully, said that Peek's milk agreements were a failure and his work a total loss. He did it so impersonally that one newspaperman remarked afterward, "That was the coolest political murder that has been committed since Roosevelt came to office."

We used to go to the big teas Henry and Ilo Wallace gave in their Wardman Park apartment, when he was Secretary of Agriculture. Later we went to their dinners. The food was delicious and as wholesome as Iowa corn, but the flowers held my attention because Ilo is an artist at arrangements. Beautiful as a flower herself, she could create a picture with iris, pink gladioli, and yellow roses. After dinner, we often went into Henry's library to sing Spanish songs accompanied by Spanish victrola records.

At a crowded White House beer party one night in 1939, I sat at a knee-high table with Mrs. Helen Essary, a newspaper columnist herself and wife of the dean of the newspaper corps, J. Fred Essary of the Baltimore *Sun*, Secretary Wallace, and Secretary of War Harry Woodring. We were jammed together behind the Marine Band and directly under Calvin Coolidge's picture. The little table holding our glasses kept moving from the contact with our knees.

Helen said, "This table is moving about like an Ouija board. Let's play it is and ask some questions. Quiet, now. Olive, you ask a question." I smiled at Henry Wallace and asked the psychic table, "Will Henry Wallace be President of the United States?" We sat there with our hands on the table. We agreed that if the table moved right the answer was yes; if left, it was no. After some indecision, it moved to the right. Henry blushed and said, "My gosh, I didn't push it."

Henry Wallace has many powerful enemies. They are forever blaming him for "plowing under little pigs" in 1933, as though he were a devil deliberately bent on doing evil to pigs and human beings. Wallace never bothered much to explain the facts of this seeming Machiavellianism of his, but Lowell Mellett, writing for the Bell Syndicate, July 15, 1944, explained the "horror tale about the little pigs." He said that in the summer of 1933 the farmers in the corn-hog states faced a desperate problem. Price of hogs, low; corn to feed them, scarce; a severe drought in the northwest section of the United States; a disappearing foreign market; everything depressed, except mother hogs, who blessed the farmers with an unusually large crop of millions of hungry little mouths to feed—with a dwindling supply of corn. Along to Washington came a subcommittee to represent the corn and hog farmers, producers, packers, and others. They had a plan. They asked the Department of Agriculture to contract the packers to purchase and process pigs weighing from 50 to 110 pounds, the product to be disposed of to the Red Cross and other relief agencies. Wallace arranged it as they requested and six million surplus pigs were turned into one hundred million pounds of pork to feed the hungry. The very tiniest porkers that could not be handled as meat by the packers became fertilizer and were, in that sense, "plowed under." If all these pigs had been held until the usual marketing age, they would have eaten seventy-five million bushels of corn. The next year the corn crop was one whole billion bushels short. Mr. Mellett said:

"I've often wondered why Mr. Henry Wallace, who, for aiding this effort to save the farmers on the one hand and feed the city folks on the other, has been labeled the exponent of an 'economy of scarcity,' hasn't spent a little time in explaining the facts to the people of America. I've wondered even more why farm leaders like Mr. Ed O'Neal of the Farm Bureau Federation, and Mr. Albert Goss of the National Grange, and Mr. Jim Patton of the Farmers Union, have been so silent on the subject."

On May 8, 1942, Henry Wallace delivered a remarkable speech before the Free World Association. No public man has said anything more important in our time. He said it with force, depth, and eloquence, pulling no punches. One classic passage suggests that Wallace meant what he said in urging that we must fight for a complete peace as well as a complete victory:

"I say that the century on which we are entering—the century which will come out of this war—can be and must be the century of the common man. Perhaps it will be America's opportunity to suggest the freedoms and duties by which the common man must live. Everywhere the common man must learn to build his own industries with his own hands in a practical fashion. Everywhere the common man must learn to increase his productivity so that he and his children can eventually pay to the world community all that they have received. No nation will have the God-given right to exploit other nations. Older nations will have the privilege to help younger nations get started on the path to industrialization, but there must be neither military nor economic imperialism. The methods of the 19th century will not work in the people's century which is now about to begin. India, China, and Latin America have a tremendous stake in the people's century. As their masses learn to read and write, and as they become productive mechanics, their standard of living will double and treble. Modern science, when devoted whole-heartedly to the general welfare, has in it potentialities of which we do not yet dream."

The daily press practically ignored this address of Wallace's until Dorothy Thompson and Raymond Clapper began writing about it. Suddenly the press and the people awoke to its importance. Washington was flooded with requests for copies. Millions were mailed out; it was printed and reprinted. It made a strong impact on the nation's thinking at a time when many said we did not know what we were fighting for.

Look back over Wallace's record from 1932 until the knock-down, drag-out Senate fight over his confirmation as Secretary of Commerce in 1945, and you will see that he overcame all his enemies. Tenacity is the key to his success. He is never personal about it. He simply believes with fanatical intensity that the United States of America can create a good life for all its inhabitants and he'll work toward that with whatever methods seem right to him, as long as there is breath in his body.

No man with overpowering pride or ego could have endured all Henry Wallace did at the hands of Roosevelt. In 1940 he lifted Wallace to the heights of the Vice Presidency, then in 1944 plunged him into political confusion by backstage maneuvering so that he lost the Vice-Presidential nomination. In 1945 he left Wallace to fight alone the bitter struggle for the Commerce Department and the R.F.C. Wallace remained ever faithful to Roosevelt, principally because Roosevelt was the voice of Wallace's liberalism. He followed that voice, he consecrated himself to the ideas on that tongue. He was the St. Paul of Roosevelt's career.

If you walked in 1938 on a burning hot summer afternoon beyond the White House, around the south end of the State Department, past the Corcoran Art Gallery and Emergency Hospital, you came to a secondhand building which had been fumigated and painted over. In a small, bare office—such as any self-respecting vice president of a third-rate corporation would be ashamed to be seen in—you would find a thin, wiry man named Harry Hopkins. His shirt would be open and a glass of ice water would be in front of him.

Hopkins was important at that moment because, for the last four and a half years, more than seven billion dollars had passed through his hands. He had given jobs to more people than any one else who ever lived, including the pyramid-building Pharaohs! You would know that he was the senior veteran of the original New Dealers—as zestful, as eager and as hopeful as when he first arrived in Washington in 1933 to take charge of relief administration for the new President.

He had been through bitter and disappointing experiences. He had been the object of more criticism and controversy than all the New Dealers combined—and that was a mouthful. He had learned that some things just couldn't be done, but he was convinced that many things could be done.

One thing Harry Hopkins was fixed upon—that was that the Federal Government had a permanent responsibility to provide work for persons who could not find jobs in private industry. He believed that the Federal Government always would have to provide work for about a million able-bodied persons, plus another six hundred thousand twilight-zone men and women who, though still able to work. could not work at the pace required in private industry.

Mr. Hopkins drove on with hopeful enthusiasm, a hard-boiled, practical sentimentalist. He always said, "Hunger is not debatable." By nature, he has always been cocky and tough, and his vocabulary has survived unexpurgated. He did not allow criticism of relief measures and the multitude of enemies he made to get him down. When Al Smith said that nobody would shoot Santa Claus just before Christmas, Mr. Hopkins out of a fullness of experience observed, "The h-e-l-l they won't! Santa Claus really needs a bulletproof vest."

Mr. Hopkins retained a buoyant lightheartedness, not unlike that of President Roosevelt. The two were extremely congenial because their ideas harmonized, and Hopkins was never gloomy or bowed down with alarm over the state of the nation. They first met in 1928, when Mr. Roosevelt was running for Governor of New York. Mr. Hopkins was helping in the Smith presidential campaign. Both the President and Mrs. Roosevelt took an immediate fancy to him; and if he had any stronger friend during the stormy days of the New Deal than the President, it was Mrs. Roosevelt.

When Harry Hopkins became Secretary of Commerce in 1939, he struck out with great effort to bring an understanding between big business and the government. He bit into the problem, refusing to use such vague standards as "cooperation" or "confidence," because words were no test for the specific job that was needed to bring them to understand each other's functions. For instance, he got specific information about the problems of electric power, the problems of the big steel companies as opposed to the small, independent steel companies. He made a deep study of the functions of the Labor Board. He spent a great deal of time talking to industrial leaders, giving them all the time they wanted. He let them talk themselves out, while he said little. He took many of these men in to see the President privately; while they talked in general terms of "confidence," Harry was finding out specifically about their troubles. His job was not so much to sell himself and his Commerce Department program to the business men as it was to sell his program at the White House. He tried desperately to outline policy and strategy, to cut out the dreadful misunderstandings.

Of course, one of the biggest problems was foreign trade. The good old days of individual trading between business firms of various nations had gone the way of all flesh. Our competition was totalitarian foreign trade tactics. Trade had become a government matter in Germany, Italy, and Russia. We couldn't compete with it. This confusion of policies in a new and different era confounded all relationships.

Incidentally, it is interesting to know the manner in which President Roosevelt made Hopkins Secretary of Commerce. Hopkins had always hoped to go into the Cabinet, but, when the Reorganization Bill was defeated, he gave up this hope. The Reorganization Bill would have created a new Cabinet office to handle relief. But to Hopkins' astonishment one evening Roosevelt looked up from his stamp collection and said, "I am going to throw Dan Roper out and make you Secretary of Commerce." Harry said he didn't want to go into the Cabinet on those terms. Nothing more was said about it until suddenly at Christmas-time he was appointed.

Roosevelt never told him why he appointed him nor what he wanted him to do, but Hopkins had three hunches about the reasons, which are interesting. . . . The first one was strictly personal—Roosevelt wanted to do it for Hopkins. Secondly, Roosevelt wanted to get an all New Deal Cabinet, because he saw ahead of him in 1940 the hardest fight of all and wanted to be prepared for it with a stronger Cabinet. Third, Roosevelt felt that Hopkins had done all that could be done in the Works Progress Administration and that as long as Hopkins stayed in that he was a target for attack.

President Roosevelt's humanitarian impulses were strengthened and implemented by Harry Hopkins. From him the President obtained the idea of dramatizing the one-third of our people, which he described as "ill-fed, ill-clothed and ill-housed." His persistent repetition of that theme is a result of the Hopkins influence. Behind the Great Humanitarian stood Hopkins, the Expert Humanitarian, feeding him ideas on what to do.

Harry Hopkins is an easy man to know because he is unassuming in approach and full of banter. Ray admired him very much as a skillful administrator and as a practical adviser to the President. To some, perhaps, Hopkins seemed like a manipulator of men, but the sum total of his diplomatic service to his country during World War II shows that even that quality had its merit.

Early in his career in Washington, Harry Hopkins studied Franklin Roosevelt carefully—because he believed a successful operator in government here had to know when

Roosevelt meant what he said and when he didn't. If you guess wrong too often, you are out. For example, when a delegation would appear at the White House making requests, the President might write a note to a Cabinet officer, we'll say, advising that he wanted such and such a thing done, for which the delegation had asked. Sometimes the request should and could be ignored; sometimes Roosevelt meant it must be done, *positively*. You had to know your Roosevelt. Some Cabinet officers, some politicians were clumsy about knowing where the power was at the White House. In May, 1938, that power was in the hands of Jimmie Roosevelt; later, it belonged to Hopkins himself; earlier, it had been Louis Howe, and so on. Hopkins believed it was very poor policy to be invited to Hyde Park for an informal drink or a party, pull a paper from your pocket, and ask Roosevelt to read it and sign it. That made Roosevelt mad enough to scratch you off his list. He never mixed business and pleasure. Hopkins' study of his boss profited him. In the next seven years he remained closer to Roosevelt's side than any other man, and his behind-the-scenes power became world-wide.

However, Roosevelt was aware that in order to launch progressive measures for America he was not only dependent upon his loyal guard, but he could always rely upon the unwavering strength of such men as the great "Fighting Liberal," Senator Norris.

When every personality in Congress has been weighed and evaluated, a liberal cannot truthfully fail to judge

George W. Norris of Nebraska as the greatest of them all. For 40 years, first in the House of Representatives and then in the Senate, he was the finest, most far-seeing servant of the whole people of the United States we have had. No one can be cynical about him, his record, or his creed. Norris never fitted the pattern of a politician, yet he was the most successful one, with the possible exception of Franklin Roosevelt. He wore no scenery, scorned patronage, blurted out everything he thought, taunted his party machine, even campaigning at times against it. Throughout it all he flourished politically.

Labels do not always accurately describe the contents of the bottle, but it is no misrepresentation to tag Norris as a friend of the common people. He was born one of them, on a not too prosperous farm in Sandusky County, Ohio, about the time the Civil War began, and he has lived as one of them. When he was small his father died, and his only brother was killed in the Civil War. As soon as young Norris could handle a hoe, he was hired out to the neighbors. He went to school when he could, studied at night, became a country school teacher and endured privation in that miserably paid profession. He worked his way through Baldwin University and Valparaiso University and studied law outside. Then he moved to Nebraska.

Recalling the early days of his public career, Norris said, "I came to Washington a regular Republican, a strong party man. The first thing that commenced to open my eyes was a discovery I made soon after reaching Washington. In my campaign for Congress I had circulated the speeches of a Republican congressman. They sounded fine to me, and I flooded my district with them. I had never seen the man. On becoming acquainted with him in Washington, I discovered that he had never made a speech in Congress in his life, that the speeches I circulated under his name had been put into the *Congressional Record* and I found out that he was a machine politician who was made chairman of the Congressional campaign committee because he was the best man to get campaign contributions from corporations.

"And very soon after this, another thing happened. A bill was up to increase the salary of the House doorkeeper. I thought he was getting enough as it was, so I made my first speech against that bill. I spoke only five minutes, but that speech queered me with the Republican management of the House. The doorkeeper never spoke to me after I made that speech. My House patronage was cut off. I served ten years in the House after that, during eight of which my party was in power, and in all of that time I never received one single piece of House patronage. I didn't even get to appoint a page or an elevator man, not a single thing. I was an outcast from the time I made that speech."

Before long, Norris encountered the first demonstration of Speaker Cannon's grip on the House, which he was later to break by a sensational coup. The Public Buildings Committee met, and the question arose as to whether there should be a public buildings bill at that session.

"I was a greenhorn and didn't know much about how

legislation is put through," Norris said. "Somebody in the committee asked if the Speaker had been seen about the public buildings bill, saying there was no use trying to do anything unless the Speaker was for it. One member—a Democrat—moved a resolution that the chairman of the committee be instructed to see the Speaker and report whether he would let our committee have a bill. I wondered why the devil a committee wouldn't dare report a bill without seeing the Speaker. I was told that the Speaker controlled the House, and if he didn't want the bill we might as well quit. And he didn't want it, and that was what happened."

A few weeks later came Washington's birthday. The Republicans wanted to go on working all afternoon, and the Democrats wanted to declare a holiday. Norris was the only Republican to vote with the Democrats.

"I was all alone when I stood up on the Republican side," he said. "I knew that every eye was turned on me and that I was regarded as a renegade, not only by my Republican colleagues but by most of the Democrats. It was exceedingly humiliating to me, and it required all of the courage I possessed to stand up and be counted. I walked out into the cloak room and sitting there was a Republican leader smoking a cigar. We were alone.

" 'Young man,' he said, 'didn't I see you voting with the Democrats?' I answered in the affirmative. 'Well, if you expect to stay here you might as well learn now as any time that you must always follow your leader. Your life here will be short indeed unless you take this course.'

"I told him that I was going to be my own boss."

The leader replied that a good many young men had tried to buck the machine and failed. Norris, smarting, walked over to the Senate Chamber and there found the Republicans taking the stand which he and the Democrats had taken in the House.

"That cheered me up a great deal," Norris said. "I made up my mind right there that the House ought to represent the people and not the leaders."

Norris went along in his own way for several years, frequently being in difficulty with the group headed by Speaker Cannon which ruled the House. Resentment at Cannon's arbitrary tactics grew slowly among House members. Finally in March, 1910, came the historic uprising which broke his power.

Norris had been waiting for weeks with a resolution in his pocket proposing a change in the House procedure, so that the powerful Rules Committee, which dictated what legislation the House should take up, should be elected by the House instead of being a creature of the Speaker. The Speaker was not to be a member of the Rules Committee.

A ruling by Cannon on another point gave Norris a precedent for offering his resolution as a privilege motion. The Republican Old Guard was stunned. It stalled for time, and during the ensuing two days and nights of continuous session every regular Republican was rounded up for the critical vote. The Democrats and a group of Republican insurgents threatened to cast a majority of the votes, and the regular Republicans wired all members who were out of town, brought in sick members from their beds, and refused to permit a single member to get out of reach. Finally the vote came and Norris won.

Cannon offered to resign and there was a vote on that. Norris refused to vote to oust Cannon, declaring that the fight was against the system, not against Cannon personally. The motion to unseat Cannon failed and was seized upon by the Old Guard as a vindication of the Speaker, although Norris voted in favor of the Speaker.

"After this fight, even my presidential patronage was taken away from me by Taft, and I couldn't appoint a single postmaster," Norris said. "This patronage was turned over to one of the Nebraska Senators. I then decided to run for the Senate and defeated the Senator who had the patronage.

"I don't kick about being denied patronage. It is one of the things necessary to keep the machine together. It is one of the sinews of war and it is one of the things a man who has a conscience has to give up. Sometimes it is embarrassing because it puts the politicians who are looking for jobs against you."

We used to see him in the Senate, plain, unimpressive, average sized, a man one would never pick out in a crowd. Yet when he led the fight against Cannon he endured two days and a night without sleep, without changing clothes, without any food. To him we owe countless forward-looking reforms, but I think the greatest of all his many contributions to our modern democracy is the Tennessee Valley Authority. In that one project, under the magnificent leadership of David Lilienthal, is expressed the achievement of man over environment, of waters used to benefit a valley and a people.

In the past fifty years we had many individual giants in Congress to whom every one rushed to listen when their significant voices were raised in a speech. Today the Congress boasts none such, and doubtless it is healthier for the nation that this is true. We don't need prima donnas as much as we need students of government, men who will study and work to make democratic government function. The changes in the world outmode these exciting individualists. We need men who can work in unison, who know how to use the techniques of conference, the advantage of research.

Chapter Seven

A MIDDLE-SIZED MAN
TAKES ON THE CHAMP

THE REPUBLICANS BEGAN TO LOOK FOR A candidate in 1935 who could defeat "that man in the White House." They had not been able to build up any national figure whose abilities could compete with the "more abundant life" appeal of Roosevelt.

Ed Wynn, the comedian, explained their dilemma by a story of his travels in Egypt. He came across some workmen digging in a pile of ancient ruins. Wynn asked if they were digging for King Tut's tomb. "No," one of them replied, "we are trying to dig up a Republican to run against Roosevelt."

There was Hoover, of course. A friend slapped Hoover on the back, saying he thought Hoover should have the nomination because "we can't beat somebody with nobody." Hoover snapped back: "The Democrats did in 1932."

The newspapermen knew Hoover hadn't a chance. Ray was one of the first to suggest in his column the able Governor of Kansas, Alf M. Landon, as a Presidential candidate. Landon, who had put his state on a pay-as-you-go basis, was as Kansan as we ourselves were. He was realistic and full of common sense. He looked not at all as the public was then inclined to think a President should look. He was of medium height, wore glasses, and spoke with a mid-western twang. He had a charming wife and three fine children. He lived in the center of the United States, and in addition to a balanced budget, he had given Kansas a sane, progressive administration. He was a small oil well owner and operator and was a "gentleman farmer," if we have such a thing in Kansas.

Landon was easily nominated at the Republican Convention in 1936 and started out boldly there and then to make a fight for an honest, progressive platform against the reactionaries of his party. He commenced his campaign by doing a lot of missionary work among business men. He knew that many of the reforms the New Deal had made were long overdue and should not be repealed. He understood that conditions had changed in the world and that we could never go back to the old days and the old ways.

Landon hoped to convert business men to a program of moderateness. His criticism of the New Deal was at first largely aimed at poor administration. He had a "we can do it better" attitude.

Sometimes he felt frustrated. "Most businesses," he said, "are not managed by their founders but by men who have spent their lives as employees. They are not hard to deal with nor are they ruthless with labor. It is the big lawyers who misadvise big business."

Not only Landon but other men in public life condemned

the rule of the powerful corporation lawyers over business men and management. Roosevelt, himself, had a phobia on the subject. These lawyers were somewhat in the same position as the lawyer in the opera, "Porgy and Bess."

You remember Bess wants to get rid of Crown, and the lawyer appears to sell her a divorce. The price, he tells Bess, will be one dollar—that is, provided there are no complications. If there are complications, the price will be higher. Then he starts to fill out the papers and asks Bess when she married Crown. Bess says she never was married to Crown. For a moment, the lawyer is taken aback. Then he gets a bright idea and says, "That's a complication. It'll cost you twenty-five cents extra. Now, for a dollar and a quarter I change you from a woman into a lady." And he hands her the divorce.

So with the big lawyers. Sometimes they magnified difficulties with labor and with government.

Landon was unknown to the mass of the voters. His organization was too loose, in spite of the fine efforts of John Hamilton, Chairman of the Republican National Committee, upon whose shoulders rested the immense job of reorganizing the Party practically from scratch.

Our presidential candidates must charm the radio audiences, interest the casual citizen with humor, appeal to the serious with intellectual brilliance, and at all times be safely religious. If he has any time left to ponder the hard problems of the nation's welfare, he is extraordinary.

Landon had voice teachers and camera teachers, all manner of advisers. The Republican National Committee hired Ted Bohn, a specialist in appearances before the camera. He had coached Hoover in 1932 and Roosevelt for two years before he ran for the Presidency. He taught Landon to thrust out his chin and snap his head up and to "button up a smile." That last was important, for a smile is no good unless it is buttoned up—that is, unless you close it. Don't just leave it there! Close and open it. Poor Landon made a mistake in smiling in a picture at the Liberty Bell in Philadelphia, instead of looking serious and statesmanlike. He made a fatal faux pas in another picture. He was wearing an American Legion hat. He waved it while holding his regular hat in his other hand, an unconvincing gesture to the Legion. Landon's square face was not photogenic. His eyeglasses had square-cut lenses instead of round ones, which would have softened the angles of his face.

He was taught when in a crowd he should stand slightly ahead of every one else to seem to dominate the crowd, and that when riding in an open automobile he should display himself by leaning forward with head and chin thrust forward. Perhaps the worst handicap of all was that he lacked glamor on the radio. His opponent, on the contrary, had the greatest radio technique and voice of the age.

Landon asked Ray in to see him one evening in Portland, Maine, after his speech there. It was one of his early, well-balanced speeches. He had maintained that the NRA had gone too far, demanded that Roosevelt say whether he proposed to revive it or not.

"How am I doing?" Landon asked.

Ray said, "Alf, you are conducting a campaign designed to preserve your self-respect. It will leave you with a good record."

Alf said, "Win or lose?"

"Yes, win or lose—whichever way it goes—you will retain your self-respect if you make a hard-hitting campaign along progressive lines."

"That's the way I want it to be," Alf answered.

When Ray indicated he thought Landon ought not to keep the Old Guard Republicans around him, that the reactionary elements of his party were a millstone around his neck, Landon asked, "Who else can I get?"

His staff quarreled among themselves; and Landon, in the final stretch before election, joined the hysterical cry that the Administration was undermining the American form of government. Ray was disturbed because Landon allowed himself to be persuaded to stir up violent and ignorant prejudices. The Old Guard Republicans hammered at him and screamed for blood. He had started out saying that some of the New Deal was good but it must be saved from its own excesses, from its waste, extravagance and mismanagement. He ended on an excessive bogey-man scare to win votes. He alienated all common sense voters. He developed few ideas and lacked initiative.

It hurts me to write critically of Alf Landon. He was a dear friend of ours, visiting in our home, bringing gifts to our children. Personally, he meant more to us than all the Roosevelts put together.

As Landon, with a sore throat and deep weariness, drew close to the finish line, Ray again joined his train in Baltimore, en route to New York. Landon asked, "What do you think about it now, Ray?"

"About what, Governor?"

"The election, of course," Alf said.

"It's hard to tell, but it looks to me as if it is going decidedly against you."

Landon argued and quoted editors who had told him he was riding up in the clouds, and was sure to win. Ray said, "Governor, it is obvious they haven't broken the bad news to you. As your friend, I cannot mislead you. I've been traveling with Roosevelt and with you. This election is a landslide for Roosevelt."

Visitors boarded the train and began to tell Landon how he'd carry New York with a majority in Brooklyn and a million-vote majority upstate, so that in spite of the loss of New York City he'd carry the state by 750,000. Then they began talking about how Roosevelt was a Communist. They infected Landon with their scare propaganda.

Finally Ray couldn't keep still any longer, and said, "That's terrible to spread that stuff."

Landon said, "Why?"

Ray answered, "Because it isn't true. Roosevelt isn't a Communist, and you know it."

Landon said, "His policies are leading to dictatorship.

When a President gets hold of the purse strings, you have dictatorship."

Thus, in a welter of misconceptions, blindness to reality and over-confidence, Landon's campaign disintegrated.

While in New York, Landon drove out to Oyster Bay to pay his respects to Mrs. Theodore Roosevelt. As the cavalcade of fine motor cars sped along, they passed thousands of WPA workers along the highway. These poor men watched this luxury stream past. They knew it was the Republican candidate's party. They didn't know that most of the cars carried newspapermen—not rich Republicans. When they reached Oyster Bay, a New York newspaperman said to Ray,

"I think I made a lot of votes for Franklin Roosevelt back there on the road. Every block or so, I'd lean out of the car and yell to those men, 'Get to work, you lazy so and so's!' They probably thought I was a Republican politician."

Roosevelt didn't need much help from any one. In contrast to the week of cheap ballyhoo at the Democratic Convention, a hundred thousand persons gathered under the open sky in Franklin Field, Philadelphia, to hear his acceptance speech. They were not noisy, wild, or hysterical, but deeply sympathetic. There was no brassy band playing *Hail, Hail, the Gang's All Here*, but the Philadelphia Symphony Orchestra was playing a Tschaikowsky symphony. Then tiny Lily Pons sang *The Song of the Lark* to the vast thousands. She lifted that audience into breathless enchantment. It was ready for Roosevelt as he entered to the orchestra's stately *Pomp and Circumstance*. It was his floodtide. As Ray wrote:

"With a voice never more confident, never more commanding, never warmer in its sympathy, Roosevelt played upon his audience with one of the most skillful political addresses of our time. It was more than a feat of showmanship. It was a work of art which all of the political instincts of the Roosevelt dynasty were summoned to aid.

"Economic royalists. . . . We have conquered fear. . . . Privileged princes of new economic dynasties. . . . The Spirit of 1776. . . . The flag and the Constitution stand for democracy, not tyranny; for freedom, not subjection; and against dictatorship by mob rule and the overprivileged alike. . . . The enemy within our gates. . . . We cannot afford to accumulate a deficit in the books of human fortitude. . . . Divine justice weighs the sins of the coldblooded and the sins of the warmhearted in different scales. . . . This generation of Americans has a rendezvous with destiny. . . . It is a war for the survival of democracy. I am enlisted for the duration."

Roosevelt rode triumphantly in veteran style throughout the campaign.

He drove hours in an open automobile under a drenching rain and dismissed it as a trifle with the remark, "I don't mind having my shoes full of water, but I don't like to sit in a bathtub with my clothes on."

A near tragedy occurred before that speech in Franklin Field. A ramp had been built from the spot where Roosevelt would dismount from his car to the main platform. He could not climb stairs because there was no bend at the knee possible when his braces were fastened to hold him upright. His son, Jimmie, had hold of his arm, supporting him. On the other side, Roosevelt leaned on a cane. Suddenly the brace on his left foot, not properly fastened, gave way. Roosevelt collapsed sidewise, crumpling beside Jimmie. The unexpected and very heavy weight threw Jimmie off balance. Roosevelt didn't fall completely down, for ready hands nearby helped Jimmie pull him up.

His papers scattered, however. When they were picked up, their order was mixed. Roosevelt, panting and disturbed by the narrow escape, responded to the crowd's ovation as he came up on the platform. No one in the audience knew of the episode; it was dark and the ramp was hidden from the massed thousands.

Roosevelt began sorting and rearranging the pages of his manuscript. He expected Vice President Garner to speak for at least five minutes ahead of him. But Jack was not in too good form. He kept repeating a sentence or two but couldn't get going on a speech. He gave up the whole business, said, "I present to you the President of the United States," and sat down.

Clutching his disarranged speech, Roosevelt took his place at the microphones. The crowd's long ovation gave him time to finish the rearrangement of pages and to recapture his poise.

That speech was one of his greatest. The whole 1936 campaign showed him at his best as a politician. Operating experimentally and with great latitude, he did not stay in any one place long enough for his opposition to fire at him. He was always way out in front with ideas, leading, educating, putting on a marvelous show.

While Landon was trying so hard to win votes, Roosevelt was moving among crowds that exceeded anything in history—crowds that pressed about his automobile or train, murmuring, "I almost touched him." On one trip, a care-worn poor man, in an excess of emotion for this champion of forgotten men, tossed his watch into the automobile. Roosevelt implored the police to locate him and return it.

Day after day, in the east, the west, the north, the south, through seas of unknown thousands, he was accorded the greatest popularity ever attained by any President. He remained human, approachable. Once, pausing during a speech from the rear platform of his train, he explained, "I'll have to wait a minute; there's a grand kid fight going on down here."

The campaign, however, was not entirely without a boner. In Bloomington, Illinois, speaking from the rear end of his train, Roosevelt said, "I am glad to be back in Bloomingburg." Senator Jim Ham Lewis turned to Mrs. Roosevelt and said: "What a delicate tribute to Horner." Horner was the Jewish candidate for reelection as Democratic governor.

The masterful Roosevelt touch was not as effortless as most people think. "Missy" Le Hand, Roosevelt's secretary, told Ray that the President after a speech would modestly ask, "How'd I do?" He was never sure of himself; although seemingly very assured, his hand frequently trembled and he always exhibited nervousness before a speech. Before his Madison Square Garden address in the 1936 campaign, his tension was almost unbearable. He thought the applause would never stop, yet he had not wanted to emulate Landon by calling, "Mr. Chairman, Mr. Chairman," because it sounded plaintive and ineffectual over the radio. As he stood there, he felt he just couldn't go through it.

No matter what the man felt, there was seldom any doubt left in the mind of his audience. In his "We have only just begun to fight" speech in Madison Square Garden, he said, "The very employers and politicians and publishers who talk most loudly of class antagonism are already aliens to the spirit of American democracy. Let them emigrate and try their lot under some foreign flag in which they have more confidence." It sounded like an ominous challenge. What Roosevelt probably meant was, "Let the rich who don't like it here go abroad, take a look around, and they'll find they are better off here." Close advisers, however, said he meant what he said and wouldn't care if they all left the country. Whoever wisecracked, "Roosevelt has a 'whim of iron,'" was probably right.

He had a lot of enemies. Stories swept the country, like the one about a famous psychiatrist who died and, when entering heaven, had the following conversation with St. Peter:

"You were a famous psychiatrist on earth, were you not?"

"I was."

"You successfully treated Alfred Smith when he had illusions of greatness and thought he was Solomon, didn't you?"

"I did."

"You successfully treated Father Coughlin when he thought he was the world's greatest economist, did you not?"

"I did."

"You successfully treated Huey Long when he thought he was Napoleon, did you not?"

"I did."

"Well, you're just the man we need up here now. You see, we've been having trouble with God lately—he thinks he's Franklin D. Roosevelt."

Labels were pasted all over Roosevelt. Orators cast him in every role in the political catalogue—some said he was a Hitler or a Stalin. In one and the same breath, they denounced him as a Socialist or a Communist. Extreme left-wingers said he was a gay reformer doctoring his patients with bread pills. Al Smith accused him of "taking the country to Moscow." Norman Thomas wailed he was taking socialistic policies out—on a stretcher. The greatest roars of anger and outrage came from the great capitalists. They really hated him, in spite of the satisfactory economic statement of the National City Bank of New York that "business activity was at the highest level in more than five years and signs of recovery were more widespread than at any time since 1932."

A few rich men did support Roosevelt. One such man,

when asked why he was voting for Roosevelt, walked over to a map on the wall and, pointing to Europe, said, "Where else would I have been so well off?"

It is history that Roosevelt won the election, carrying every state except Maine and Vermont. He had told friends he could make a better campaign against himself than his opponent, because he knew his own weaknesses. In his pre-election guess, he grossly underestimated his own majority.

"Missy" Le Hand thought 1936 would be Roosevelt's last campaign trip. As they left the White House to go to Hyde Park to cast their votes, she looked back at the White House with tears in her eyes, feeling as though they were leaving for good. On election night, she said Roosevelt never did make any comment; he never said, for example, "I'm elected." Only once did he question the returns. That was when the New Haven returns came and he said, "Those must be wrong; they couldn't be that large." He worked impersonally over the figures.

A month later, he said it was hard to realize what the election meant and the responsibility of it. But "Missy" surmised that had he been re-elected by any less majority than in 1933, Roosevelt would have felt his policies were not vindicated. He considered the big job was to get the New Deal machinery running smoothly so that it would carry on after he was gone. The large Democratic majority in Congress bothered him because some crackpots rode in with him who, he feared, might try to shove through some bad legislation. The veto would be an important lever. He was more worried about this left-wing fringe of his party than the rightist opposition.

Right after the 1936 election, Frank Sullivan wisecracked in the *New Yorker* that it was time for the Republicans to be careful; that they ought not to let all of their men run for the Presidency but should save some of them for breeding purposes.

When the Gridiron Club held its winter dinner after the election, Alf Landon came to Washington and made the finest speech of his career—packed with humor and good sportsmanship. Roosevelt also spoke. When told before the dinner that Landon was coming, Roosevelt said, "Good— that's fine. Maybe we can have a good-will atmosphere. That would be a good thing."

Alf Landon didn't go back to his oil wells and farm and forget about his responsibilities as Party leader. He wrote to my husband:

"There is a big job to be done, not for the sake of the Party but of the country. . . . I cannot feel that Roosevelt's irregular methods, his short cuts, deal competently with the questions he has raised."

And further: "I do not believe the Jeffersonian theory that the best government is the one that governs the least can be applied today. I think that as civilization becomes more complex, government power must increase; but it is something to be approached slowly, with caution, not with inertia but with competency. We have had too much of the slap-dash, jazzy method. I do not think there is anything new or revolutionary about the redistribution of wealth theory. Every wise statesman in every period of history has been concerned with the equitable distribution of prosperity in his country."

Ray replied: "I must say that at times Roosevelt disappoints me very much, and this is one of those times. He has let the labor situation get completely out of hand and has thrown his administration too much to the labor side. If ever a man deserved to lose a strike, it is Tom Girdler; and yet I think, indefensible as his course is, public sentiment is more with him than it is with John Lewis at the moment. Roosevelt's genius is in developing issues and breaking the ice, but at times he does not show the balance which is needed to keep things on an even keel. Until recently labor needed a friendly hand at Washington, but now it is more than able to take care of itself—and Roosevelt should function as a stabilizer. He has made little or no progress toward budgetary balance. His efforts to develop his social legislative program have been erratic. Likewise he has messed up his tax evasion case by trying to make a Roman holiday of it; rather than either trying his test case in the courts, or else dealing with the question in a normal, legislative way—instead of this form of Tory hunting."

I remember so well another letter from Alf, written June 14, 1937, in which he told how he had been drilling a well in eastern Greenwood County, Kansas. He worked until 10 o'clock the night of June 9 and left the rig to go home, tired, dirty and muddy. He had to open two wire gates to leave the oil well property. He had no trouble opening them, with the light from the headlights of his car, but fumbling around in the dark to close them was difficult. He had to grope along the barbed wire, through the wet grass, to the accompaniment of a storm—with flashes of lightning and rolling thunder—to find the lock of the second gate. He snagged his finger on the barbed wire. He was hungry and tired. Suddenly he thought: "My God! This time a year ago I was being nominated for President of the United States."

Chapter Eight

SHALL WE NEVER
BE RID OF THE PAST?

I WENT UP TO THE CAPITOL TO HEAR Roosevelt's second inaugural address. This time it was January, instead of March, for it was the first inauguration after the passage of the Lame-Duck Amendment. Cold rain drenched me and as soon after Roosevelt's speech as I could, I picked up my car at the garage and hastened home to find Ray already there, sitting comfortably before a roaring fire in a huge bathrobe, eating a delicious lunch from a tray.

"I got to the office," he said, "but when I began to sneeze and sniffle, I decided not to go to the Hill for the inauguration. So I came home, got undressed and listened to it on the radio. Gosh! The networks do a fine job of coverage. I'll bet I know more about the inauguration, sitting here, than you do."

Since he had had an advance of the speech, he could write his column comfortably by the fire. We enjoyed the rare freedom of an afternoon by the fire and went over to Donald Richberg's for cocktails.

Don pointed out that any second inaugural speech (he

had spent the last three days at the White House helping to write this one) was an historic occasion by tradition, calling for a traditional statement of philosophy; that Roosevelt was speaking to millions at home and abroad who do not follow politics closely and who hear him but seldom, if ever, at any other time. Therefore, the speech had to be general; but every word was carefully weighed and packed with significance. He said they labored to get away from the use of the word "God" in the ending, yet to include the usual divine touch. They finally decided upon "divine guidance."

Don told Ray that Roosevelt was annoyed at a piece Ray had written saying that Roosevelt hoped an era of good feeling with subsiding strife and anger would mark his second term. Ray had written that Roosevelt had pilloried the economic royalists, mussed the hair of sedate Tories, thrown rhetorical brickbats through the windows of well-warmed clubs, but that he really didn't like quarreling—and he wanted a pleasant, friendly atmosphere. This column angered Roosevelt because, he said, he had never thought there could be an era of good feeling—it was hooey to think you could have it in a period like this. There could be no good feeling either at home or abroad. At home, the sit-down strikers held huge automobile plants practically as hostages; there was argument within the heart of the New Deal over the Supreme Court; big business hated the President; Congress was sourly bickering; and the "more abundant life" was as far away as ever. Abroad, civil war raged in Spain; Italy had conquered Ethiopia; the Japanese were expanding in China; and Germany's intentions to conquest were growing.

Immediately after Roosevelt's second inauguration, excitement and fury spun the wheels of government. We had a ringside seat, and a close-up view of Roosevelt's attempt "to pack" the Supreme Court. The tale is typical of Franklin Roosevelt, who, you will remember, always described himself as a quarterback of a football team. Sometimes he used a forward pass; the next, a line plunge or a lateral, depending upon what seemed the most promising play of the moment. This time, he used a forward pass—but he failed to get Congress out there on the receiving end in time.

Future students of American history probably will ponder that year and that play. Their verdict may be like the one expressed in *The Education of Henry Adams*—"That any road was good that arrived."

By 1937 the Supreme Court had smacked down much of Roosevelt's dearest New Deal legislation, calling it unconstitutional. Roosevelt—and, for that matter, Congress too—was hamstrung by a "horse-and-buggy" Court of nine "old" men. Of course, these nine men didn't all disapprove of all the New Deal legislation. Brandeis, age 80; Stone, age 65; and Cardozo, age 66, approved; Chief Justice Hughes, age 74, usually approved; Roberts, age 61, agreed part of the time. Thus there were five of the nine about whom no great complaint could be made. But Van Devanter, age 77; McReynolds, age 75; Sutherland, age 74; and Butler, age 70, were accused in Roosevelt's language of blurring "new facts through old glasses, fitted as it were, for the needs of another generation."

The Supreme Court, having finally moved out of its dingy room in the Capitol Building into its fabulous eleven-million-dollar marble temple across Capitol Plaza, in 1934, was a noble sight for visitors to behold. I will always remember my own shocked dismay when I first came to Washington in 1917, to see the Supreme Court, the very top of our government, chambered in a basement room of the Capitol that smelled old and neglected. When they moved to their new palace, Justice Brandeis expressed regret and said he would much rather the Court continued to use the little room off the corridor which connected the House and Senate Chambers, because "our little courtroom kept us humble."

Justice Stone commented to our friend, Ned Bruce, as he showed him through the new building with its grandeur, pink marble pillars and red plush curtains, "We'll look like nine black cockroaches when we get into that room."

Confident in the prestige of his ten million majority at the polls, Roosevelt began to search for a method to streamline the Supreme Court. A few days before the judiciary dinner at the White House in February he was in no friendly mood. To a friend, he said, "I've got to have them to dinner. I don't know whether to grin and bear it or take myself three old-fashioneds before I go downstairs and blow my breath in their faces."

He dropped his judiciary bomb, however, at a press conference, 10:30 A.M., February 8. As the newsmen arrived at the White House, they noticed a long line of Cabinet and official cars. Was a special conference going on with some members of Cabinet, House and Senate leaders, and the Chairman of House and Senate Judiciary Committees? Probably wages and hours legislation, correspondents thought. The air was tense and every one sensed something unusual.

Inside the President's office Roosevelt said, "I have something very important for you today." This was an extraordinary opening, and there was none of the usual joking between the President and the men in the front row. He then told the newsmen that he had come to a very definite conclusion that some reorganization of the judiciary was required. He was sending a message to Congress that day, which he sketched through for the press. His voice betrayed excitement, his mood was bright and buoyant. While he obviously realized the historic importance of the occasion, there was nothing solemn about his message. Laughs rang out as he took sideswipes at the Court. He emphasized that the Constitution puts it up to the President to make recommendations concerning all legislation. This he was doing as a basis for discussion. The draft will save Congress the "trouble of trying to put the language together." This got a big laugh.

He told the history of changes in the size of the Court. As every one knows, the Court has been altered by Congress several times in our history; in 1789 it had six members, seven in 1807, ten in 1863, was decreased to eight in 1866, and increased to nine in 1869.

With a twinkle in his eye, he proposed "the appointment of additional judges in all Federal Courts, without exception, where there are incumbent judges of retirement age who do not choose to retire." While he spoke of all Federal Courts, the crucial point was to swell the Supreme Court up to fifteen members if the septuagenarians refused to resign.

When the proposal reached Congress and was sped by radio and telegraph all over the land, screams of outrage and denunciation poured into Washington. He is violating the Constitution, he is too clever, he is seizing control of the last citadel of the law, he wants to be a dictator—screamed the opposition.

Tom Stokes, the brilliant Scripps-Howard correspondent, wrote a graphic story of how the Supreme Court itself received the news:

"It looked like just another day of arguments before the Supreme Court.

"The nine men were in their places on the bench, outlined against the heavy curtains behind. The court room was half-filled with spectators. A New Jersey lawyer was addressing the Court.

"He did not know, none of the spectators knew, that they were witnessing a historic occasion, an hour shadowed with tragedy that none on the bench would confess, except to himself.

"The lawyer perhaps did not notice the mimeographed

sheets which Chief Justice Charles Evans Hughes was intently reading.

"The document engaging the Chief Justice was the message of the President, then being read to Congress, which had some not pleasant words to say about aging Supreme Court Justices, and which proposed that if they did not retire, younger men be appointed to the Court to help them with their work.

"Presently the Chief Justice finished with his copy. He moved restlessly in his chair. Then he handed the copy to Justice Willis Van Devanter, at his right. Expressionless, this consistent opponent of the New Deal read the message.

"The lawyer talked on. Chief Justice Hughes appeared to fix his attention on him, but you could imagine that his mind was elsewhere.

"Spectators sat listlessly. Occasionally, one or two rose and left, and others slipped in.

"With quiet efficiency, a court messenger boy distributed copies of the President's message to the Justices who had not seen it.

"Justice Pierce Butler hunched his big shoulders over the document. He is 70, and no friend of the New Deal.

"Next to him sits Justice Louis D. Brandeis, who is 80, one of those who have stood by much of the Roosevelt regime. He glanced at the mimeographed sheets, switched on the desk light in front of him, and began to read intently. His fine features were silhouetted by the light.

"Justice Butler meanwhile had finished reading and

turned to chat with Justice Roberts. The portly Butler began to chuckle. He and Roberts seemed to be enjoying the situation.

"The ascetic-looking Brandeis finally concluded reading and settled back, his full head of hair a bristling crown against the back of the tall chair. Thus he sat, in contemplation, for a few minutes. Then he picked up the message and began to reread it, occasionally rubbing his ear.

"Meanwhile, Justices James Clark McReynolds and George Sutherland, anti-New Dealers, and the two other Justices, who like Mr. Roberts are under 70—Harlan Fiske Stone and Benjamin N. Cardozo—had perused the President's words.

"The Chief Justice presently conversed gravely with Justice Van Devanter, who smiled grimly once or twice.

"Brandeis completed his second reading and turned to chat with Van Devanter. The latter waved his arm once in a gesture denoting impatience. Brandeis smiled occasionally.

"The reading was finished up and down the line.

"Routine returned again.

"But a pall seemed to have dropped down along the bench. Words hung in the air, words from those printed pages:

" 'This brings forward the question of aged or infirm judges—a subject of delicacy and yet one which requires frank discussion . . . Perform their duties to the very edge of the grave . . . In exceptional cases, of course, judges, like other men, retain to an advanced age full of mental and physical vigor. Those not so fortunate are often unable to perceive their own infirmity.'

"Six men beyond 70—of what do they think?"

How was it Roosevelt sprang his plan when he did and in the way he did? Homer Cummings, then Attorney General, told Ray the genesis of the plan about as follows. Shortly after the election the President said he wanted to do something to bring the Court into line with the sentiment of the country but he didn't know how to do it. He asked Cummings to put his department to work to study all practicable plans, schemes, history, et cetera. They made a list of possible solutions. Gradually, after study, they eliminated all ideas except one which was far down on the list. Of the President's immediate staff, Samuel Rosenman and Donald Richberg were consulted in the final stages, but Tom Corcoran and Ben Cohen were not in on it at all. The Justice Department assembled figures, material, and drafted the bill.

Why didn't they try to get a Constitutional Amendment, Ray asked? Cummings said, "Why change the Constitution to correct an improper or incorrect interpretation of it? The Constitution is all right—why change?" He thought it would take too long a time to get an amendment to the Constitution. Lots of state legislatures are Republican and would refuse to pass an amendment. If thirteen governors refused to submit the amendment, it was dead. Everyone who has been around a legislature knows how easy it is for vast and powerful moneyed interests to buy up legislatures to prevent action. In any case, an amendment would take a year or two. Labor unrest doesn't wait. It increases. Sit-down strikes, a new weapon of labor unions, were springing up in industrial centers. The situation was already acute. . . . And, anyhow, we don't want to change the powers of the Court or clip its wings, Cummings said.

The proposal was sprung in the early part of the Congressional session to give plenty of time to get it through the current session. If the bill passed quickly enough, nominations of new members could go to the Senate at once. The bill had a thirty-day clause after enactment, too, which would give the overaged Justices time to resign. Some of them might wait to see if the bill passed before resigning. If they still stayed on after passage, they would have to take the responsibility for enlarging the Court. In that way, the Court members themselves would determine the size of the Court.

The Attorney General also stressed the need to get the whole matter cleared up early so that Congress could proceed to other legislation, shaped with the knowledge that it would receive unbiased consideration when it came before the courts.

My husband supported the Roosevelt court proposal in his column. To the hysterical cries of the critics, he pointed out that every strong President in a period of great change and crisis had evoked similar vituperation. Here is a quote, for example:

"We saw the executive power grasp in one hand the sword and purse of the nation and in the other the legislative and judicial authority and hold them in a relentless grip to the complete annihilation of our constitutional rights . . . The superb Constitution under which our country has grown great and respected is torn in shreds."

That quotation was written not about Roosevelt, but about Lincoln in 1862. The same has been said of every strong President. . . . Of Washington:

"The President has violated the Constitution."

Of Jackson:

"Jackson has shaken the Government to its foundation, violated the Constitution."

Of Theodore Roosevelt:

"One who so lightly regards constitutional principles, and especially the independence of the judiciary, one who is so naturally impatient of legal restraints and due legal procedure and who has so misunderstood what liberty regulated by law is, could not be safely trusted with successive presidential terms."

A strong man always meets a crisis with the practical tools at hand. Maybe they aren't the best tools, but they are available—which is all-important. Sometimes, instead of a strong man, you draw a Buchanan, who wanders helplessly between two worlds—one dead, the other powerless to be born. Or you get a Hoover. Then even the conservatives begin clamoring for a Mussolini, who will act and get on with the business in hand. All the President sought to do was to break the paralysis the Court had brought about, when certain of its members refused to cooperate in streamlining our system to a new age.

Roosevelt lost the fight when Congress denied his proposition, but, as the years rolled on, destiny gave him his chance to remake the Court. All but two of the old Court either resigned or died, and Roosevelt, one by one, appointed seven new members . . . As a matter of fact, before these changes were made the nine old men themselves handed down several perfectly satisfactory decisions.

Justice Roberts was the particular justice whose vote switch on New Deal legislation called forth the wisecrack, "A switch in time saves nine." So many wits around Washington wanted to claim credit for this wisecrack that Ray laughingly told me, "It's a wise crack that knows its own father!"

Many of Roosevelt's advisers—like Robert Jackson, then assistant Attorney General and later on appointee of Roosevelt to the Supreme Court, who made the most effective presentation of the plan to the Congressional Committees—felt that the whole proposal had been badly handled. He said that the argument of congestion of cases before the courts was a mistake, because it was not impressive. The proposal was too big to try to put over in any guise. He felt Roosevelt should have brought it up during the political campaign or when the Court was handing down adverse decisions. Then aggrieved groups would have supported him. But no adverse decisions had been given during that term of Court, so there was no immediate excuse for the move.

Shall We Never Be Rid of the Past?

Had Roosevelt held off to see if the Wagner case or social security legislation had gone against him, he would have had a solid case.

The Supreme Court fight demonstrates that it is vital to the proper functioning of our form of government for the judiciary composed of appointed members to act as a check rein, but not as a dead weight, upon the executive and legislative departments which are elected by the people. What is more, this fight explains a great deal about Franklin Roosevelt. Here his goal was definite, justified and necessary, but his method of reaching that goal was often impetuous, badly planned and badly timed.

Midway in the year 1937, Roosevelt faced a most serious ebb in public confidence. The Macon, Georgia, *Telegraph* was urging his impeachment. Everything seemed to be going sour, and the public had the jitters—owing primarily to the severe labor troubles. Roosevelt was a lonely man. Gus Gennerich, his aide, had died; Louis Howe, his close friend, was gone. Mrs. Roosevelt was out of town so much, and the President spent night after night working alone in the White House. The world situation was close to general war. All in all, the picture was grim and depressing.

In late June, consumer goods buying fell off. By September, the steel industry started on the swiftest, steepest drop it ever experienced, from 92 percent of capacity in April to 35 percent of capacity in six months. The automobile industry was in a bad way, too. General Motors was employing only about 90,000, as against 175,000 normally. The country was in another depression, but Roosevelt called it a recession.

And strikes . . . dreadful ones in the steel mills and the automobile factories, where the new weapon of labor—the sit-down strike—was used advantageously. Congress had made collective bargaining obligatory. Industry and labor were supposed to sit together and work out disputes under the Wagner Act. But the Act did not positively compel an employer to sign an agreement with organized labor. The Supreme Court had said the Wagner Act "does not compel any agreement whatever."

Tom Girdler, head of Republic Steel, said he would sign no contract with the C.I.O. and as for the A.F.L., he would rather go back to his apple farm than to sit down at a table and bargain with them! The same attitude was taken by Youngstown Sheet & Tube and other independent steel companies, in contrast to U. S. Steel, which negotiated an agreement. This sabotage precipitated bloody warfare. Life and property were destroyed. Girdler and his ilk stood adamant on this pearl of wisdom from the august lips of J. P. Morgan, "Anybody is justified in doing anything so long as the law doesn't say it is wrong."

Labor leaders like Philip Murray were opposed to the sit-down strikes, because they endangered labor. They prevented discipline and occurred when labor couldn't afford them, at the price of public opinion.

One reason for the large number of little rebel sit-downs

in the automobile industry was the youth of the workmen;
the majority were in their twenties—a reckless age. The
speed of the work on assembly lines required the most active,
nervous type of worker, who was explosive. They were new
in unions and felt their oats. They pulled the "quickie"
strikes and were irresponsible.

Of course, during these trying times, Ray talked often
with John L. Lewis, head of the C.I.O. On July 29, 1937,
Ray had a long interview with this dramatic, bushy-eye-
browed leader of labor. He was in a pleasant good humor,
talked freely and leisurely. They talked first of labor in
politics. Lewis said it was inevitable that labor would insist upon political expression as it had in other countries.
Large labor organizations with their local forums and meet-
ings lead naturally into discussion of political questions which
concern labor. What labor would do politically at the moment, Lewis couldn't predict; but, certainly, they were going
into the 1938 elections, and they might do a little avenging
against those who—elected with labor support—had afterward turned traitor to labor.

One interesting point in the interview was Lewis's answer
to the question, "Do you think Henry Wallace, Secretary of
Agriculture, wants to run for the Presidency in 1940; and
would the C.I.O. support him?"

"Oh, he wants to run all right," Lewis replied, "as do a
lot of others. But he has 3,000 county farm agents who are
viciously anti-C.I.O., who take the viewpoint of implement
manufacturers and are anti-labor." Lewis told about getting

into a taxicab one day. The radio was on, and the C.I.O. and John Lewis were being denounced. At the end of the ride, Lewis asked the taxi driver what program that was. "The Farm and Home Hour," he replied. "That program was put on by the Department of Agriculture and shows what Wallace is doing," said Lewis sourly.

Ray asked, "Have you seen President Roosevelt lately, and have you noticed any change in his attitude toward you?"

"I've not seen him for months—in fact, only twice since election. He doesn't want to see me. . . . I'm not respectable politically right now. Roosevelt doesn't want to see people who talk frankly. He only wants those who agree with him. I tell him what I think, and it makes him uncomfortable and disturbs his equanimity."

Ray said, "Then you don't agree with the assertion often made that Roosevelt takes orders from you?"

"Roosevelt is not taking orders from me. He hasn't said a thing about the murders which federal bullets (martial law invoked in Ohio strikes) have perpetrated on our people in Ohio. He could crack down on Girdler and Grace by pulling back government contracts. Yet he does nothing. He does nothing to stop the Navy from breaking the New York shipyard strike. The Treasury Procurement Division is violently anti-labor."

He paused and frowned, then said, "I have a lot of respect for old Dan Roper. He is Secretary of Commerce, and he doesn't do a thing without consulting business and industry. When he makes a radio speech, he shows it in advance to industrial advisers. His staff people are all business people. But our Labor Department—Frances Perkins—is a non-labor department. Labor is not represented in it. It is filled with women, intellectuals and pinks."

"There's Ed McGrady," Ray said.

"Yes . . . but he is treated shamefully. He has no authority. He is not permitted to know what is going on. Clerks snicker at him when he goes down the hall. Places are filled without consulting him. No—the Department of Labor ignores labor."

Devil or saint as he may be, John L. Lewis always gives a good show. Have you ever wondered what his power would be if instead of those bushy eyebrows and that scowl he had the mild features of William Green of the American Federation of Labor? Once a friend of ours, meeting John L. Lewis for the first time, was astonished to see him smile.

"Why do you scowl in all your pictures?" he asked Mr. Lewis.

"Scowling is my business," he replied.

I shall never forget John L. Lewis at Paul Y. Anderson's funeral. This brilliant newspaperman died under tragic circumstances. He left a specific request that his funeral services be conducted by that great fighting liberal, Senator George Norris, and John L. Lewis. His friends gathered at Gawler's Funeral Parlor. When the moment arrived to begin the services, the great figure of Lewis walked slowly, dramatically to the casket, and looked long upon the face of his friend. Then slowly he began to speak, as we sat breathlessly watching. I cannot quote the exact words, but as I remember it, he opened somewhat as follows:

"Paul Y. Anderson was my friend. That makes me proud."

He continued, oh—so dramatically: "Sometimes in the night I cannot sleep. The raven sits outside my bedroom door. In those chilly hours, two events in my life comfort me. Once when I was a young man I stood beside a river and watched a man try to take his God-given life by plunging into the icy current. I jumped to his rescue, and because I was young and strong, I saved that man's life. That comforts me when the raven sits outside my door.

"Another time, this strong right arm of mine reached out to save a mother's young child from the angry heels of runaway horses. That mother's thanks comfort me as the raven sits outside my door.

"Now I have a third comfort. Paul Y. Anderson was my friend. I shall remember that too, when the raven sits outside my door."

John L. Lewis sat down and wept. I knew it was a breathlessly moving moment, and my spine tingled with awe. Yet there was a note of overemphasis, a certain phoniness that detracted from the effect. This was Paul Y. Anderson's funeral. Yet John L. Lewis talked almost entirely of John L. Lewis.

Chapter Nine

WE ALMOST KILLED
THE GOLDEN GOOSE

Bγ SPRING OF 1938, AFTER FIVE YEARS IN power, the New Deal had settled down into a bewildered middle age. Business men continued to blame the government; the government blamed business men; and labor was blaming both for the sad state of affairs, which had grown out of a kind of bloodless civil war.

Suddenly, seemingly out of the sky, but undoubtedly due to much backstage coaxing, explaining and wooing by Harry Hopkins and Donald Richberg, several groups of topflight industrialists indicated their willingness to actually sit down in Washington and talk things over with the President.

In one group was Ernest Weir of National Steel, Alfred P. Sloan, Jr., of General Motors, Lewis H. Brown of Johns-Manville, Martin W. Clement of the Pennsylvania Railroad, and Colby M. Chester, Chairman of the National Association of Manufacturers—who had been among the economic royalists who were Roosevelt's most bitter critics.

George Harrison, Chief of the Brotherhood of Railway Clerks, got this particular group together first, to show them how the railroads had satisfactorily worked out their problems with organized labor by mediation—so that they had had no strikes in fifteen years. He explained to them we were living in a new day and that, in the public interest, business, labor and government ought to learn to sit around a conference table to settle disputes. He pleaded such a logical dependency of each of the three upon the others that the five capitalists asked how to go about sitting around a table with the President. Harrison said he'd been at the White House a number of times, knew the President and would try to arrange a meeting.

Harrison, the good Samaritan, wrote to the White House, asking for a conference. A couple of weeks went by without a reply. This made all of the men a little hot under the collar. What was more, Ernest Weir was scheduled to go to Bermuda; and the others, with heavy calls upon their time, couldn't wait indefinitely to hear whether or not they would suddenly be summoned to Washington.

An intermediary was told of this odd situation and offered to try to find out from the White House what was holding up Roosevelt's acceptance of such an olive branch of peace. Was the President intent on angering these business leaders further? Was he fooling when he said in his Jackson Day speech that the White House door was open to all?

No, fortunately, nothing as ominous as that had happened. The fault lay with Marvin McIntyre, presidential secretary, who said, "Yes, the letter is around here some place in a basket. I haven't seen the Boss about it yet. I'll call you back about it."

All afternoon and evening the intermediary waited for that call, but it never came—nor did it the next day. Feeling that this was a crucial test, this friend then telephoned direct to one at the White House who, he knew, would get the message to Roosevelt—his efficient secretary, Marguerite Le Hand.

She said, "I'll tell the President at once and call you back." In half an hour, she called. . . . "The President said, 'Fine! I'll see them Tuesday at 5 P.M.'"

You would think that settled the appointment, but no! Weir postponed his trip to Bermuda, and all five men stood by awaiting telegraphic invitations to the conference. Monday afternoon came—the conference supposedly only 24 hours away. Still no telegrams to the waiting men. Another phone call to Mac—he hadn't got around to sending the telegrams. "Would it be all right to make the appointment for Wednesday?"

"Hell, no!" shouted our angry intermediary.

"O.K. I'll send them right away for Tuesday, 5 P.M.," Mac said submissively.

At long last, after all this maneuvering it was arranged. The men earnestly wanted to cooperate. During the session there was a friendly, reasonable give and take on both sides. For example, they talked about the government housing program. Brown, of Johns-Manville, said the housing program

· 141 ·

wouldn't work until they got practical men into it who knew about housing.

Roosevelt said, "You're right, and I'll tell you how it happened. Some of those working on the plan had an idea that no one who stood to profit from the program should be in it. But I realize that is wrong, because it keeps out the men with the know-how. We'll change that."

The same attitude prevailed in everything they talked about until, in amazement, Alfred Sloan leaned toward the President and said, "You mean you really want us to tell you what we think and to give you our ideas and suggestions—you really want them?"

"Of course I do," said Roosevelt. They arranged a plan whereby the industrialists could see government men handling specific business matters whenever they wished. All in all, it was a great love feast. As they left the White House, Ernest Weir, fearful of newspaper comment, would say nothing except, "I want to go to Bermuda. I want to go to Bermuda."

Three days later Roosevelt held another conference, this time with Owen Young, Thomas Lamont, and John Lewis. Still another was called, with 50 business headliners—the Business Advisory Council. In fact, a whole rash of conferences broke out, marked by a new solidarity between labor, business, and government.

Incredibly, however, between the conferences Roosevelt kicked business in the solar plexus. . . . His temperature went up as he said that $600,000,000 in holding-company hands controlled $3,000,000,000 of utilities' capital. Was he leading up to elimination of holding companies? Yes, he was. Would the President apply this to all lines of industry? Yes, everything . . . banks and everything.

Jitters, jitters, all over the place. Few could deny the evils of holding companies. But would this mean a complete reorganization in business? Just when and what would come next? It was a strange situation when a man in the White House for five years—who had been through one depression and faced another—was so uncertain of his methods that even his close advisers never knew from day to day whether he'd appear with an olive branch or a battle axe!

One explanation was that Roosevelt's advisers were split into two mutually hostile groups. The olive-branch group of men—like Donald Richberg—urged him toward closer cooperation with business, wanted him to do everything possible to induce business to pull its weight. The crack-down advocates thought that a waste of time. They expected nothing but sabotage from business. Hammer it, said they, rabble rouse enough popular support to take the whip hand politically to play the role of savior and expand government control over business—the only solution in the long run, they believed. These were the Tommy Corcorans, who viewed calmly the prospect of a smash if necessary to bring this about . . . It seemed a bad influence. For a time we wondered if Roosevelt really could pull the country out of the hole it was in.

We never knew Tom Corcoran well. I met him only once

or twice. He is a handsome Irishman with a gay singing voice. Perhaps Roosevelt, needing friendship and gayety in his loneliness, turned to this friend who was always there, guitar in hand.

Possibly Roosevelt and his advisers did not intend to make a general smash attack on business. Possibly they only wanted to free business from the restraints of monopolistic influences so that business men would have an open chance at a free market, using the government as a policeman to insure real competition.

Ray went out to Cleveland, Ohio, to see Tom Girdler, president of the Iron and Steel Institute, and asked him his recipe for business recovery. He answered, "Quit playing football—and particularly a certain kind of dirty football. . . . I have no recipe, because the situation is nothing as simple as that. We need to return to active cooperation between the government and business. Both big and little business is willing to give its cooperation, but President Roosevelt singles out the steel industry, asks us to cut prices but to keep wages the same—it just can't be done. I believe in high wages—buying power depends on high wages—but if we reduced steel prices 10 percent, all steel companies would be in the red."

Girdler was sure that the minute prices were reduced, cut-throat competition would bring wide distress and would not increase sales.

Automobile people used this same argument to defend their sustained prices. Everybody yelled for free competition but, throughout the whole business structure, a multitude of activities prevented competition and supply and demand from affecting prices. Manufacturers needing steel were compelled to pay the price agreed upon in the steel industry. Competitive bidding produced only a flood of identical prices. Competition is a religion which is preached more enthusiastically than it is practiced.

. . . "No," said Mr. Girdler, "steel prices must not be cut."

Yet a few months later, when there was a possibility that the government would look into the steel price situation, steel men went into a panic.

Ray always claimed that he broke the price of steel because one night at a dinner party Thurman Arnold, assistant to the Attorney General, rushed up to Ray and said, "Well! Here's the man who broke the price of steel. Your article intimating that the government threatened to investigate the price of steel caused Roosevelt to put a reference to it in his fireside chat. That gave Ed Stettinius, of United States Steel, who had been fighting for lower steel prices, the impetus to cut the price from $36.25 for steel billets per long ton in June, to $34 in July."

Whether or not the lowering of the price of steel in the fall of 1938 could be said to have caused the upswing is impossible to say. Maybe it was due to the rearmament programs which sprang up like dandelions all over the world when Prime Minister Chamberlain returned from Munich with his "peace in our time."

We Almost Killed the Golden Goose

At any rate, rage is what we had in the year 1938. . . .
Business and industry were enraged at Roosevelt and the
New Deal; Republicans were enraged at the vicious Democratic machines of Hague in New Jersey, of Kelly in Chicago, and of Tammany in New York. Roosevelt was enraged
at industry for refusing to lower prices and cooperate in recovery. Abroad, Hitler raged about German minorities in
Poland and Czechoslovakia, and he marched on Austria, en-
raging the western world. Everywhere this rage inhibited
intelligent action.

Then we had a midterm election, in which Roosevelt tried
to "purge" Democratic Senators who had voted against most
of his policies. He was justified in fighting for his administration and in going into Democratic primaries to root out
Democrats who rode under Party colors but voted with the
Republicans on major policy measures. All politicians understood that Roosevelt was right to insist upon general under-
lying loyalty but much bitterness developed all over the
nation against him. This was symbolized by a new rash of
anti-Roosevelt stories. One that made the rounds was about
three boys who were said to have rescued Roosevelt when he
fell overboard on a fishing trip. In gratitude to his rescuers,
Roosevelt offered to give each boy anything he wanted. The
first boy wanted a pony, the second, a motor boat. The third
boy spoke up and asked for a military funeral. Roosevelt
said, "You'll outlive me . . . why ask me for a military

funeral?" The boy answered, "When I go home and tell Dad I've saved your life, I'll need a military funeral."

Since I lived and voted in Maryland, I was particularly interested in the effort to replace Millard Tydings, Senator from Maryland, with David J. Lewis, Congressman, who had been a New Dealer before the words were coined. Like Senator Norris, Lewis was a Liberal when Franklin Roosevelt was still in knickers. It was my privilege to head up the fight for Lewis in Montgomery County, Maryland. I learned a great deal about intraparty warfare in this fight. It climaxed in defeat for David Lewis, but I learned how difficult it is to buck a smooth running political machine, ably bossed by a veteran politician. We had no organization. We had no money. We had trouble even getting our watchers at the polls.

President Roosevelt, whose political axiom was audacity, entered the Maryland Senatorial Primary, as well as the others, to demonstrate that he wanted men in the Senate who were liberals at heart. Senator Tydings had a long record of anti-New Deal votes behind him, and this had earned him the opposition not only of Roosevelt but also of Jim Farley —in fact, this was the one primary purge to which Farley brought personal enthusiasm.

David Lewis campaigned on principles of the welfare and rights of the common man. The Democratic voters, however, decided that the issue was whether or not the President of the United States could come into the Maryland "free state."

We Almost Killed the Golden Goose

They said he could not tell them whom to send to Congress. That settled it.

For me, it was a valuable experience in democracy at work; and I recalled what H. A. Tolley, AAA Administrator, had said in a speech in Atlantic City in December, 1937:

"Democracy in operation is often unlovely to behold. It creaks along over many a bump and rocky place, and, when it finally arrives, half of its load may be spilled out. But what is the alternative? The alternative is some dictatorial system like those that have sprung up in other parts of the world. If we really prefer the method of democracy to that of dictatorship, we must be somewhat philosophical about its faults at the same time that we do what we can to make it operate more effectively."

Everybody continued stubborn and bitter. After a pump-priming expenditure of some 17 billion dollars, the business cycle was down again and recovery was stalemated. Many taxpayers said that the spending program was money that went down a rat hole, to be lost forever.

They forgot some monumental dividends scattered throughout the country, such as: 40,000 miles of new highways, 19,000 bridges, 105 new airplane landing fields, 1,400 medical clinics—not to mention the great power projects of the Tennessee Valley and Boulder Dam. Perhaps we could have gotten along without any of these things . . . they were all a by-product of the business of feeding and trying to save the self-respect of men and women whose services were not needed in private enterprise.

Benjamin Franklin said, "It has been computed by some political arithmetician that, if every man and woman would work for four hours each day on something useful, labor would produce sufficient to procure all the necessaries and comforts of life; want and misery would be banished out of the world, and the rest of the 24 hours might be leisure and happiness."

Strange things had been happening all over the world that changed all values. Money had lost a great deal of its power. Rich nations, like England and France, were being brushed aside by poor nations, like Germany, Italy, and Japan. The starved "have not" nations were doing much with little; while rich nations, like ourselves, having much, did little with it.

The wheels stood still and the country milled about. Roosevelt complained bitterly that private capital would not advance money on perfectly sound, good industries that wanted to expand. The three fields in which the main load of recovery would be carried were the railroads, the utilities and housing; yet, for special reasons, none of these got going. Railroads made no purchases of steel rails because of high steel prices and wage increases; utilities did not expand because of uncertainty of government policies; housing almost stood still because of high wages and material costs.

Besides all this, the government severely reversed its spending policy from a plus of 3 billion dollars to a minus of 400 million dollars in a year. Social security taxes also took a little out of the consumption power. There were a few dollars less in every pay envelope.

Possibly Elliott Thurston of the Federal Reserve Board was right when he surmised that we'd never again have steady forward surges, only short, sporadic spurts of prosperity. Gone was the free land of the 1800's for surplus population; gone, the opportunity for great projects such as the building of the railroads; gone, the tremendous outlet for surplus capital in automobiles, radios, roads. There was the curious juxtaposition of huge bank accounts, as though we were in a peak boom, with interest rates at the lowest level they had ever been. Maybe the government would be forced to skim off large surpluses through taxation, then feed them back in forms of capital expenditures in which private industry could not engage, such as reforestation projects.

One night at dinner at the home of David Cushman Coyle, writer and economist, we argued at length about the government pump-priming to provide consumer buying. I remember Thurman Arnold, assistant Attorney General, was there—which always meant a rousing argument that cleaned cobwebs from your brain. Coyle outlined his theory about government spending. He claimed that the United States would always have to pump an average of 15 billion dollars a year back into consumers' pockets. Since there could never be public projects enough to absorb such a sum through government work, the money would simply have to be given away in pensions—or any way to get the money out and circulating.

Wouldn't that undermine people's morale, to get checks for nothing, for no work? Coyle said that was only a matter of custom, the way people looked at it. If every one received checks, rich and poor, lowly and powerful, no stigma would be attached to it—just as there is no stigma attached to receiving public school education.

How could you finance it? By a stiffer income tax, Coyle said. Considering the rebellious attitude of taxpayers, we argued that they would not stand for taxation severe enough to recoup 15 billion a year. It will have to be done gradually, he said. Ray and I were horrified at the idea, predicted rebellion and dire psychological effects. Thurman Arnold was inclined to philosophize that there was a possibility that we wouldn't be able to lick our problems . . . France did not seem able to. Maybe we would sink down and go the way of France, passing through many futile, aimless years. It was all very depressing.

The struggle between men and machines was symbolized in the story of a rubber plant in Ohio, which stood untouched and unused for a long time, an idle monument to the fight over mechanization. The manager of the mill had installed an electric eye similar to that which automatically opens the doors in the Pennsylvania Railroad Station in New York. The electric eye is always open, it never wanders, it never makes a mistake. Such a device was hooked onto a masticating mill to count the number of times the operator of a particular machine slashed the rubber as it was ground between two huge steel drums. The rubber needs to be chewed and chewed in this mill to make it more plastic. The more plastic it becomes, the better automobile tire it makes. To facilitate the chewing process, the operator must slash the rubber as it winds over the rollers and double it back. The operation is fast, heavy and dangerous. About 15 knife slashes are required on each batch of rubber to insure adequate plasticity. The electric eye would give the management an automatic count of each knife slash, thus insuring a written record of the operation, to prove that the rubber had been sufficiently worked. But when the electric eye was attached to the machine, indignant workmen objected. They refused to work under this mechanical watchman. The management had to shut down the mill. It remained idle, a symbol of the rebellion of man against the machine.

Many factors entered into the labor troubles of this period. The fight was not always over wages and hours. Frequently it was resistance to the speed up, or a matter of jurisdictional disputes.

Great hope had been placed in the Wagner Act, which guaranteed to labor the freedom to organize and to bargain; but the trouble with it was that many people thought the National Labor Relations Board, which the Wagner Act established, could prevent strikes and labor disputes. But, as President Roosevelt pointed out when he signed the Wagner Act, the National Labor Relations Board did not act as mediator or conciliator in labor disputes.

We Almost Killed the Golden Goose

Collective bargaining does not end labor trouble. Sometimes it made both sides more bitter. After labor has been organized there is still the problem of bringing about peaceful adjustment of differences. There must be extensive facilities for voluntary arbitration. Notice should be given before a strike is called, to allow the government time to investigate and to attempt to bring both sides together.

Of course there were some happy adjustments in individual plants. In 1929 J. C. Hormel, president of a meat-packing company in Minnesota, distributed a new product—canned chicken. Orders rolled in until dealers were stocked up, then sales dropped. Hormel started to cut his payroll. One employee, when told he was no longer needed, blew up. "You can't do that to me," he said.

"Can't do what to you?" Hormel asked.

"You can't turn me out in the street," the employee said. "You couldn't turn a horse out in the street. You can't do it to me."

"You can go back where you came from, can't you?" Hormel said.

"No," replied the employee, "I had worked up a little peanut stand in our town and I was making nine or ten dollars a week. You came along and said you would give me $20 a week to can your chickens. I supposed you would keep it up. I didn't think you would keep me here a couple of months, ruin my business and turn me out in the street."

That episode bothered Hormel a good deal. He began turning over in his mind the picture of what his firing of men was doing to the community. Some of his men told him they were stuck with installment purchases and would lose furniture or other property if thrown out of work. He had the only large industry in Austin and he saw that his layoffs would affect retail business throughout the town. It was a heavier responsibility than he wished to have laid at his doors, so he began searching for some means of steadying employment in his plant.

Out of this was born his idea of an annual wage. He guaranteed his men fifty-two pay checks a year, covering also vacation and sick leave. Well, it wasn't quite that simple. Fearing to bite off more than he could chew, he tried the idea out in one department. Employees became suspicious and it was dropped. Later employees asked that it be revived. More than 2,000 of his men were on the annual wage. His plant had been organized by the C.I.O. a year and a half before. Hormel said that hadn't changed anything except that several of the men had to go away to attend union conventions.

On the weekly wage, no check on hours was kept except for information purposes. The men had a certain amount of work to do. They were paid so much for doing it and when they were through they could go home. As a result they did forty hours' work in thirty-five or thirty-six hours and had the extra time for their own. Work was budgeted by departments and excess production carried a bonus. The budgets were fixed by collective bargaining, with considerable wrangling. Men were alert against being squeezed in this way. But both the men and Boss Hormel seemed satisfied with the results.

When production was down, Hormel, with a fixed wage cost, was forced to use his ingenuity to find new work. That is why he went into the canned soup business as a sideline. The arrangement made his job harder because he couldn't meet a dull spell simply by dropping men. He found that on paper the scheme cost him $300,000 a year. But he still had the money in the till and found that it had been made up in various ways. For example, if a department saved 10 or 15 percent on operating time, some of the overhead costs—like electricity and water—were less. Anyway, the earnings were not affected.

So Hormel was satisfied. His employees were given one year's notice before a layoff. When asked if he would carry his men through a whole year if business fell off sharply, he replied, "That's what we do with our vice presidents, and we try to give all our men the same treatment as vice presidents."

Not all manufacturers were as farsighted. We had so much bad news about unemployment, labor troubles, and political suspicions, we forgot some of the good news . . . for example: 43,000,000 Americans had *not* ceased to work at regular jobs; over 30,000,000 owners of automobiles had *not* ceased to consume daily 60,000,000 gallons of gasoline; 10,000,000 people had *not* ceased to go to the motion pictures daily; they had *not* stopped spending almost $1,500,-000,000 for tobacco and cigarettes; millions of Americans

were *not* worrying about the safety of more than $57,000,-
000,000 deposited in the banks; American citizens were *not*
failing to spend $4,000,000,000 on annual vacations. This
was my husband's favorite statistic . . . approximately 99
percent of American business men had *not* issued statements
blaming the government for business conditions. And,
further, that the 1 percent who had blamed the government
were not worried about being leaned up against a stone wall
and liquidated!

For five years we had had uncompromising Tories and
uncompromising New Dealers. It made a spectacular battle;
but, in the end, under our form of government, it settles
down to give and take. Eventually there is a compromise.
New Dealer Jerome Frank said in his book, *Save America
First*, that life could not go on without halfway measures
and "gradualness." When you use an automobile brake on a
hill, you are practicing "gradualness." The brakes that had
been put on—such as stock market controls, banking regulations, wages and hours legislation, Social Security, unemployment insurance—were the "gradualness" of our government brakes upon our economic hill.

Chapter Ten

WASHINGTON PARTIES
ARE SERIOUS AFFAIRS

IT IS TRUE THAT SOCIAL LIFE IN WASHING-
ton frequently influences the business of government—seldom in a sinister way, but in the manner of congenial friends
meeting often who like to do favors for each other. Therefore it is usually important to entertain and be entertained
by people in influential positions, if you want to succeed in
politics.

Although the average newspaperman and his wife are not
usually invited to diplomatic parties, chiefs of newspaper
bureaus and columnists are often included. When Ray and I
first began to see the inside of some of those magnificent
houses on Sixteenth Street or on Massachusetts Avenue,
where Ambassadors and Ministers from foreign countries
live, work and entertain, I could not feel at home or at ease.
These fabulous houses are beautiful and filled with old
world treasures. I hated the dull, stilted protocol that went
with dinners and luncheons. My excuse to myself for slack-
ness in social duties was that we held no official position, were
just plain midwestern newspaper people and could add no

distinction to formal parties. I didn't know that often diplomats and their staffs are lonely, or that only through their contacts with Americans do they learn about our country. I too could benefit and increase my acquaintance of the world by knowing them and, through them, something of other countries.

At first we went shyly to the large receptions at the embassies. The first dinner we attended was at the Italian Embassy. I paraded into the dining room on the arm of a young diplomat who had arrived in the United States only two days before. At the table I chatted in English to my dinner companion, who seemed very dumb because all he did was smile and nod. I had just concluded that he didn't speak English, when he burst out, "Have you ever seen bananas growing?"

No, I admitted, I had not. I could not figure out what that question had to do with my conversation about the elegant new marble Supreme Court Building on Capitol Hill.

Pompously and very slowly, he launched into a detailed account of how bananas grow, their uses, the climate most satisfactory for them, and shipping methods. When the ladies retired, leaving the men to their coffee and cigars, another lady asked me, "Did you learn about bananas, too? I sat beside that new attaché at dinner last night." She told me then that the young man spoke no English but, in preparation for his diplomatic duties in the United States, had memorized an English translation of an article on bananas.

Latin American hospitality was showered upon me one morning when I went with Mabel Vernon, Chairman of the

Washington Parties Are Serious Affairs

Peoples Mandate Committee, to talk with two different South American diplomats about peace and Western Hemisphere friendship. Appointments had been made for us a week ahead of time. When we were ushered in to the first legation, at 10:15 A.M., we saw, to our horror, that their idea of American hospitality was to serve American cocktails at that time in the morning. To show our appreciation we felt we must drink at least two. We managed that but were completely overcome when we found the same hospitality at the next legation. When we escaped after two additional cocktails, we fuzzily decided we had contributed our share to good neighborliness, and went home to sleep it off.

It was somewhat difficult for me to become accustomed to the objective attitude sometimes displayed in Washington social life. Hostesses in Washington who are ambitious for social success often do strange things. I shall never forget a telephone call a friend of mine received from one such ambitious lady who chirruped: "I hear your husband is about to be appointed to a Cabinet post. If that is true, won't you both come to dinner next Tuesday evening? If it isn't true, do come in for coffee afterward."

Officials particularly, and sometimes even newspaper people, have to be careful about accepting invitations from propagandists and lobbyists of special interests. We once accepted an invitation from a stranger in town because she mentioned a Senator who was a good friend of ours. He and his wife would be present, the hostess said, as well as an outstanding Justice of the Supreme Court and a prominent Congressman. We all accepted and enjoyed a delicious dinner. Later, several of us happened to drive home together. The Senator said, "Say, exactly who are these people who entertained us? They invited me, saying the Clappers were coming, so I was sure it must be all right." One by one, we all confessed to the same bewilderment. These particular strangers turned out to be fine people, but it was a little terrifying to think how effective the technique could be in unscrupulous hands.

On the other hand, a hostess can often bring together people of divergent views to a more rational attitude toward each other. This is the theory that motivates Evelyn Walsh McLean, whose wealth and fame are well known. She believes that friendship is the greatest force on earth. Unhesitatingly she will invite to her dinners people of violently opposed viewpoints. They are then seated together in the belief that if they can really get to know each other they are bound to be more tolerant. During the bitter isolationist fight, Senators Burton K. Wheeler and Robert Taft were seated alongside Senators Pepper, Guffey, and Congressman Sol Bloom, ardent interventionists.

Evelyn McLean's dinners are real events in Washington. It is exciting to see one or two hundred guests of prominence assembled in her great drawing room. Flower-bedecked tables seating eight to twelve are spread throughout several rooms. The many-coursed dinners are served by caterers on gold plates and exquisite china while an orchestra plays soft music. It is all done in the grand manner and you feel as if your generous-hearted hostess wants nothing else in life except to have you attend her dinners and enjoy yourself. She accepts almost no invitations in return, and since she has everything in the world money can buy, the only thing her friends can do to please her is to accept her invitations.

I know from personal experience, however, that promoting tolerance by making antagonists dinner companions does not always work. It happened that several times at Mrs. Mc-Lean's dinners, I had been seated beside a southern gentleman who expressed violent opinions against the Negro race, was opposed to education and equal employment opportunities for them, and advocated that the southern states of the United States should again secede from the Union if the north continued its misunderstanding of the place of the Negro as a slave. We argued violently. I became so upset by his undemocratic attitude that I found it difficult to be polite.

When for the third or fourth dinner I found myself again beside him, I turned to the man on the other side of me, who was a mild little stranger, and said: "Do you mind if I talk to you all the time during the dinner? I thoroughly dislike the man on my right and do not wish to talk to him."

He looked astonished, but gallantly agreed to accept my undivided attention. We talked for several minutes, until suddenly the lady on his left said to him, "Do you mind if I talk to you the remainder of the dinner? I hate the man on my left so much that I refuse to talk to him at all. We disagree so violently I am apt to pick up this squab and throw it at him."

Washington Parties Are Serious Affairs

Our poor little Mr. Milquetoast gulped a couple of times. However, he met the challenge and kept both of us in good spirits during the rest of the dinner until we dispersed to the drawing room where Mrs. McLean usually entertains her guests with a first showing of a moving picture.

Evelyn McLean does do a great deal of good. You hear about her great society dinners, but you seldom know of her generosity to a multitude of civic and charitable projects which could not function without her help and her personal attention. Every week since our war casualties started to come to Walter Reed Hospital, she has entertained one hundred wounded servicemen at her home. Each man is asked to bring his wife or sweetheart. They are entertained just as lavishly as are the brasshats at her other parties.

At one White House formal dinner, I had the pleasure of being seated beside Alexander Woollcott. He was a great tease. "Missy" Le Hand, whom he adored, sat opposite him. Woollcott started to light a cigarette after the soup course. "Missy" leaned over to tell him he was not allowed to smoke at State dinners until coffee was served.

"Who says I can't smoke?" thundered Woollcott. "Who'll stop me?"

Poor, lovely "Missy," embarrassed, said, "It just isn't done, Alec. Be a good boy, please! This is the White House."

"Well, who'll stop me? Will the President come over here and take it away from me? There is not another house in this country where I can't smoke if I want to. It is bar-

baric. . . . Or will one of the flunkeys snatch it from my mouth. . . . Or will one of the Secret Service arrest me? I'm going to do it just to see what happens."

All through dinner he kept a cigarette out, frequently making threatening movements to light it. "Missy" was miserable in anticipation, but he never actually lit it.

He regaled me with many stories, but I like best his descriptions of visits to see his dear blind friend, Helen Keller, to whom he thoughtfully took, not roses or flowers, whose beauty lies chiefly in color which she couldn't see, but great bunches of geranium leaves, which gave spicy, fresh fragrance that appealed to her two senses, smell and touch.

A hostess in Washington whose invitations we never declined is Mrs. J. Borden Harriman. Born in old New York's Four Hundred, she never played the society game; but her influence among the powerful in Washington for 40 years is incalculable. At her famous Sunday Night parties we found only those who were doing worthwhile things. Brilliant, imperious, a powerful and handsome woman, she used to announce after the servants had cleared away the dessert, "There is Scotch and water on the sideboard. Please help yourselves. And now, Mr. Ambassador, do tell us what you think of the debt moratorium." From then on, the evening would be dazzling as Senators, diplomats, writers, and artists argued under her inspired questioning.

She has a genius for drawing people out of their conversational shells and because she knows everything that has happened in Washington in 50 years, she can always pin down a man or an idea. They seldom escape her vivisection. Her keen interest in life and people make her irresistibly loved.

Mrs. Harriman began dabbling in politics as one of McAdoo's willing workers at San Francisco in 1920 and at Madison Square Garden in 1924. Because of her interest in politics, she often is bracketed with the other famous hostess of Washington, Alice Roosevelt Longworth. But they are not much alike. Alice was born in politics. Mrs. Harriman acquired her interest in it. Alice is a playful spectator who was just frivolous enough to run up to Elihu Root after the 1912 Republican Convention and shout, "Toot! Toot!" to remind him of the steamroller which he had helped drive in reducing her redoubtable father, Theodore Roosevelt, to the proportions of a corn fritter.

Mrs. Harriman takes her enthusiasms more seriously. In 1912, at the Democratic Convention at Baltimore, she became so impatient as she hung over the gallery rail nibbling a chocolate bar and drinking pop, that she undertook to break the Wilson-Clark deadlock by going down to Charley Murphy, the late Tammany chief, and inquiring earnestly, "Why aren't you for Wilson?" Charley was so violently opposed to Woodrow Wilson that he was unable to find words fitting to address a lady on the subject.

In 1937 President Franklin Roosevelt appointed Mrs. Harriman United States Minister to Norway, "land of goddesses and heroes." Her popularity there was climaxed by her courageous actions when the Germans sailed up the Skagerrak and the lights of Norway went out. Mrs. Harriman drove into exile with the King and his government. Later, she escorted Princess Martha and her children to the United States.

We used to be invited frequently to fashionable Crescent Place for dinners or Sunday luncheon at the magnificent home of Eugene Meyer, owner of the Washington *Post.* Once Mrs. Meyer kindly asked us to bring our children, Janet and Peter, to Sunday luncheon. Peter was only seven years old, and his red head barely topped the dining room table. I was talking to Mr. Meyer when he suddenly arose hastily, dashed around the table, knelt down, and put his arm around Peter. Silent tears were coursing down Peter's face as he contemplated a huge pink lobster that had been placed in front of him. Peter had never had a lobster to eat before, and he was frightened about how to eat it. Mr. Meyer said, "I don't like them either, Peter. Take this away," he ordered the butler, "and bring in some roast beef for this boy. We are having ice cream for dessert," he comforted Peter as he wiped away his tears.

I never paid any attention to protocol when I wanted to entertain any one. It is a regrettable fault. To me, these people were interesting in their own right as individuals, and I liked to invite them, not because of rank, but because they were friends who would enjoy a couple of carefree hours together. Such was my intention when I invited a group to a picnic luncheon on our outdoor terrace one Sunday in early June.

I asked that scholar and philosopher, Dr. Hu Shih, who

was at that time the Chinese Ambassador. I had also asked two Justices of the Supreme Court, Harlan Fiske Stone, with his kindly, wise little wife, and the delightful bachelor of the Court, Frank Murphy. That was bad, my protocol experts told me. You could never seat the Justices properly with an Ambassador present.

"But it is a picnic," I said; "they'll sit at scattered tables, wherever they please to light."

"A picnic," chorused my horrified social experts. "You can't mean a picnic—so informal for such distinguished guests. It is unthinkable. You'll find they won't come."

To further confuse everybody, I asked a Cabinet member, Attorney General Robert Jackson and his charming wife, Irene. Also there were present two members of what might be called the secondary Cabinet—Paul V. McNutt with his wife, Kathleen, and Thurman Arnold, with his wife, Frances. There were others, too: among them, the former Governor of Pennsylvania, Gifford Pinchot and Lelia Pinchot, the Eugene Meyers and Stanley Hornbeck, Adviser to the State Department on Far Eastern affairs (now Ambassador to Holland), and his energetic wife, Vivien.

To my delight, picnic or not, all those invited came. The first headache I encountered was that the extra servant I had expected failed to show up. Lelia Pinchot rescued me by bringing in her chauffeur, who helped with the serving. The plates were served from the buffet in the dining room, then the guests walked out to sit wherever they chose.

I was the last to step out onto the terrace. There were no

place cards, no orders at all to any one as to his place at the tables, but to my astonishment I saw that every person had seated himself or herself exactly according to protocol. A place had discreetly been left for me at the hostess end of the first table, and on the right of that, sure enough, there sat the Ambassador. The Supreme Court had accommodated itself at a small table seating only four people. Unquestionably correct. The Cabinet and sub-Cabinet had discreetly appropriated another table out under the trees. In short, those who really ranked had automatically taken their correct places.

Every one relaxed finally to eat fried chicken, ham, potato salad and all the good things my cook had provided. We had a good time, even though we talked about the ever more alarming approach to war.

Next morning, my butler brought me a man's fine felt hat which one of the guests had forgotten. The initials inside were H.S. I thought of course it belonged to Justice Harlan Stone, and drove at once to his house to return it. His butler looked at the hat and denied that it belonged to the Justice— too small for his extraordinarily large head size. I puzzled a while over the H.S. Suddenly it came to me. It belonged to Ambassador Hu Shih, and I hastened to the Chinese Embassy to return it.

When a newspaperman becomes president of the famous Gridiron Club, that exclusive group of 50 men who twice yearly give a magnificent dinner in Washington, he rates as a social lion and is widely entertained in deference to the club. Attending the dinners are all the political "importants" —the President, his Cabinet, many heads of bureaus, Senators, Congressmen and of course diplomats from other countries who always marvel at the spectacle of a group of free newspapermen kidding and roasting the leaders of this government in humorous skits and songs.

Ray was elected president of the Gridiron Club in 1939. The president is expected to open each dinner with a three-minute speech delivered to its distinguished audience in total darkness. The witty and sarcastic speeches of the president of the Gridiron Club set the pace for the dinner and must be delivered verbatim, which doesn't allow for any adlibbing in case the president flounders. Although he was an experienced lecturer, Ray found it difficult to speak in the dark, even for three minutes.

I waited up anxiously to hear the report on the rehearsal, the night before the show. Ray was in a complete state of jitters, repeating over and over again, "I can't do it. I can't do the speech in the dark." I rehearsed it with him several times and made him go to bed. He was in just as sad a state at breakfast the next morning. Our sixteen-year-old daughter Janet started teasing him but, when she saw the seriousness of his anxiety, she firmly said to him:

"Daddy, this is ridiculous. You have the great honor of being president of the Gridiron Club. You cannot let them down tonight. I will give you the same instructions that my dramatic teacher at school gave to me. This is what you

must do when you get up tonight to speak in the dark. . . .
First, plant both feet firmly on the ground, dig your toes
in as though to clutch the floor for support. That gives you
a firm foundation. Next, stick out your chin. Next, open your
mouth and let the words flow out. It's easy. . . ."

Her father didn't pay very much attention to her and
began hunting all over the house, collecting curious things—
a tiny flashlight, a piece of black cloth, a piece of pasteboard,
which he made into the form of a small tent. Upon inquiry
I learned that his intention was to rig up a little tent in the
dark, under which he would place his notes for the speech,
and, in case of emergency, could flash on the flashlight and
follow his notes.

When he arrived at the Willard Hotel that night, he first
received President Roosevelt for cocktails. The President
said, "How are you?"

And Ray said, "Nervous. I'll be better after the speech
is over."

The President told him that he had never gotten over
nervousness before speaking. If you were close enough to
watch him, you could see his hands trembling. He said that as
soon as he heard his own voice, he was all right. He tried to
reassure Ray.

The five hundred guests gathered in the banquet hall and
the band played, *There's Music in the Air*, as the lights
gradually faded out. Then began Ray's awful moment. Suddenly he remembered Janet's advice, planted his feet firmly
with toes digging into the floor. He stuck his chin out. He

already had his glasses on, his notes before him in the little tent, and he held the flashlight in both his hands over his papers, ready to switch it on. But as soon as he made his salutation, "Guests of the Club and Candidates for 1940," the audience laughed and he felt completely at ease. The speech gave a witty insight into the affairs of the world at that moment, as well as a prologue of the skits for the dinner.

Mrs. Eleanor Roosevelt, taking pity upon the "Gridiron Widows," those wives of men who were left alone on Gridiron nights, always invited us to the White House on those nights. She loved stunts and skits, too, and could whip together in no time at all very clever shows in which Cabinet ladies and White House secretaries took part. Newspaper women and Gridiron Widows were expected to do their share of entertainment. We took our play acting very seriously and would agonize to produce amusement and wit.

Mrs. Roosevelt, too, added to the merriment by telling personal anecdotes. One I liked best was about the time that she made a purchase in a store and told the clerk to charge it to Mrs. Franklin D. Roosevelt, the White House, Washington, D.C. The girl took it down carefully. At the end she looked up and carefully inquired, "Any room number?"

Among famous hosts in Washington were the Woodrings. One of their parties I shall always remember. About 10 P.M., I sat gaily talking to Marvin McIntyre, the presidential secretary. I was telling him an amusing story about his favorite song, *Carry Me Back to Old Virginny* . . .

Madame Dressler, the American widow of General Dressler of the Polish Army, had been asked to sing over the Polish radio in celebration of American-Polish friendship. The song she intended to sing was *Carry Me Back to Old Virginny*. The interpreter announcing the song to the listening Polish audience translated it as follows:

"Madame Dressler will sing an old American folk song entitled, *Carry Me on the Back of an Old Virgin.*"

I was midway of my story when the Secretary of War hastily crossed the room to us. "Mac," he said, "I have some bad news for you—you are wanted at once at the White House. The Japanese have sunk the American gunboat, *Panay*." Practically every man at the party—including the Secretary of War and other high-ranking officers—left immediately for their respective posts, since no one knew but what this might mean war with Japan immediately. In just such a manner, serious notes often creep into Washington social gatherings.

Chapter Eleven

SWING YOUR PARDNERS
IN THE WHITE HOUSE

O NE MAY EVENING IN 1937 WE WERE invited by Mrs. Roosevelt to the White House to learn again an old dance, the Virginia Reel. She had always wanted to see this graceful old dance done in colonial costumes in the East Room and had decided that the White House spring party for the newspapermen on May 28 would be a fitting time to have it.

Five newspapermen and their wives—the Jay Haydens, the James Lloyd Wrights, the Fred Essarys, the Ulric Bells and the Clappers—joined Mrs. Roosevelt, her brother, Hall Roosevelt, James and Elliott Roosevelt, their wives, and the President in the East Room at 8:45 P.M.

Except for Mrs. Roosevelt, I doubt that any of us had danced the Virginia Reel since we were children. Our husbands had complained bitterly about going, but none could refuse Mrs. Roosevelt.

She was waltzing energetically with her brother Hall when we entered, although she had returned to Washington at 5 A.M. that day from one of her trips, written her column, kept half a dozen appointments, and taken a horseback ride. The President was seated watching them and turned to greet us.

"Hello, Ray," he said, "how's old 40 percent Clapper?"

Ray asked, "What do you mean, Mr. President? Am I 40 percent wrong or 40 percent right?"

"Oh, you are usually only 40 percent wrong," he teased. The President obviously meant he wrote against the New Deal 40 percent of the time.

Ray laughed and said, "Well, I think I'm only 25 percent wrong."

"Now, Franklin," chimed in Mrs. Roosevelt, "don't start anything." She lined us up for the dance.

The President's spirits bubbled as he called out the changes in the dance, "Do si do" and "Swing your pardners." The music was accelerated, and we whirled and dipped to our partners at a furious pace until we were gasping. We stopped only when we couldn't go on any longer, the ladies dropping onto pillows at the President's feet and the men sliding, like boys, across the highly waxed floor to sit cross-legged beside us. Beer and lemonade were passed to us, and every one was at ease, laughing, joking, chattering—like any group at any newspaperman's house, speaking spontaneously of whatever came to mind.

We discussed the abdication of Edward VIII for "the woman I love" and the coronation of King George V of England. The President said that in naming the United States delegation to the coronation he got away with something

that nobody caught. He had named James Gerard, who was
hated in Germany, where he had been Ambassador when
World War I broke out; General John J. Pershing, who led
the A.E.F.; Admiral Rodman, who commanded our naval
forces in the North Sea in World War I.

"All three of them are anti-Nazi," Roosevelt said, "and
nobody mentioned it—but don't think the British didn't get
it," he added.

His eyes twinkling, he said he wondered where the Duke
and Duchess of Windsor would live. "The place next to ours
at Hyde Park is owned by Archibald Rogers. When he
died, his children, who include Herman L. Rogers, host to
the Duke of Windsor, wanted to sell or rent the estate. The
carpenters and plumbers are hard at work on it, and I wonder who might be coming to live there." He put his hand
to his ear like a mischievous gossip. "If the Duke should
move in, it would save the newspapers thousands of dollars,"
he kidded. "The same reporters could cover both of us!"

I laughed and said to the President, "Suppose the Duke
went into politics in New York. That would be a joke on
you."

He waggled his finger at me, "Yah, yah. I know what
I'd do. I'll run him for Congress against Ham Fish."

The talk switched to Germany, and Roosevelt told of
Hans Luther, the retiring German Ambassador, calling to
say good-bye. Roosevelt had said to him, "You folks can't
go on much longer. You haven't any gold."

Old Hans, as the President called him, disagreed. "Inside

Germany," he said, "it doesn't matter whether the mark has any gold behind it or not, nor what it is worth in gold. We can regulate that. Our only trouble is getting foreign exchange."

When Herman Schacht, the German financial wizard, saw Roosevelt some time before, he had said, "No, Mr. President, we won't go broke in six months—we can continue indefinitely without any currency backing at all, as long as we are self-sustained."

Going on from those remarks Roosevelt said to us, "I don't think any of you have ever heard the real story about my German Mark Company."

Eagerly, we leaned forward to hear it because during his first campaign there had been a lot of whispering gossip about Roosevelt "robbing American investors" in German marks during the 1920's. He told us how an old German-American, a member of the Stock Exchange, had told him that the German mark was going down and down, probably to zero, and that thousands of Americans who had been speculating in it would lose all they had. He wanted Roosevelt to organize a company to take all these German marks and invest them in shares, equities, et cetera, in Germany.

Roosevelt looked up the laws and found that no state in the United States permitted any company to issue shares in marks, the idea being to sell stock in marks, rather than in dollars. But he found that there was an inactive Canadian company called "United European Investors, Ltd.," organized for a similar kind of brokerage business. Shares of this company could legally be sold in New York. Roosevelt and his associates bought the name and the corporation for the cost of incorporation—$500—and set up in business. They sold several million dollars' worth of shares. German marks went down and down and, of course, as they slid, it took more and more marks to buy a share. When the mark reached three cents, the company decided to quit. When the whole thing was liquidated—the marks having been converted into German equities as fast as they came in—each American investor got six dollars for each one dollar he had put into marks. "That's how American investors were robbed," Roosevelt said, sarcastically refuting his accusers. He said he worked at this part time for four years and got $10,000 for the whole job.

Next we discussed the Soviet Union and conditions in Russia. Here Mrs. Roosevelt told of a recent conversation she had had with a strong partisan of Russia, who told her that the Stalin regime was endeared to the people because it was impossible for a worker to lose his job. He could be demoted, but he couldn't be fired. The government was the employer. Jimmie Roosevelt said, "Maybe they can't fire you but they can stand you up against a wall and shoot you. Personally, I'd rather be fired."

His mother answered, "Yes, unfortunately, that seems to happen sometimes, but it isn't a part of the theory."

The President said, "That's one means of creating a vacancy," which got a big laugh from all of us, apropos of his Supreme Court fight.

Then the President got onto a subject that was one of his favorite peeves at this time—tax dodging. Taxes were not coming in as they should, so the Treasury was investigating and uncovering amazing dodges to avoid income taxes. For example, they found some rich boys incorporating their yachts and even turning over enough securities to finance the operation of the yachts too!

One retired American Army officer had pulled a very slick evasion. This man had invented a gadget that was bringing him large royalties. To avoid United States income tax, he applied for citizenship in Canada. Then he incorporated his company in the Bahama Islands, a Crown Colony—where the taxes on his gadget were easy. Although his profits came from sales of his product in the United States, he could thumb his nose at the Treasury's prying tax collectors.

Roosevelt said many of the big boys were using similar devices. It "burned" him up because under the existing laws it was impossible to get at them. He felt the attitude that he could attack only through arousing public opinion was dishonest. He cited Andrew Mellon's tax return, showing a $250,000 gift of art treasures to the public art museum in Pittsburgh. A bright young tax investigator went to the museum and, expressing an ardent interest in art, asked to see these gifts of Mr. Mellon. The curator said they were not on exhibition. Next, the young investigator pulled a stunt "worthy of a cub reporter," Roosevelt said. He went to the Mellon house, posed as a plumber or something, and got in.

Sure enough, hanging on the walls of Mellon's own home were the works of art he had listed as gifts!

After we left at 10:30 P.M., that stimulating Sunday night, we tried to sum up all we had heard. We felt that Roosevelt —harassed and angry as he was at Big Business, at the delays in the courts, at the baffling foreign situation and other troubles—had indicated clearly only contempt for dictator regimes. He certainly expressed no envy of them. He had expressed no admiration for the speed at which they could get things done. Quite the contrary, in fact. Toward the end, he had spoken quietly and in substance had said: "Sometimes I don't like the looks of things abroad. We may be in for some very bad times. But as I read history, we have found here in this country a pretty good way of living. Where else in the world would you be able to find a group such as we form here tonight—newspapermen dancing in the home of the Executive? We've had a good time. Tomorrow some of you in the course of your work will criticize me and the government. That is healthy democracy. It is a pretty good system we have."

With his cigarette cocked in its holder in the side of his mouth, he lifted himself by his arms and transferred himself into his wheel chair. "Good-night, all," he called, as an aide wheeled him away.

That evening's rehearsal of the Virginia Reel was great fun; but, when the real performance was put on at the party, we sweltered in rented colonial costumes, the men in satin knee-breeches and lace fichus under satin coats. By some strange coincidence Ray ended up opposite Mrs. Roosevelt and consequently was her partner. She put her heart into the dance and whirled Ray about with great vigor. With his satin coat torn at the shoulder seam, his lace fichu hanging by only one pin, one leg of his satin breeches undone at the knee, he staggered off the floor when the dance was over. "Jesus, she almost killed me," he panted.

About this time the whispering stories about Roosevelt's health began to crop up. Finally, at a confidential off-the-record press conference, Roosevelt hit back. He said his relations with the press had always been good; that he believed in a free press—wanted it to continue—and never questioned the right of reporters to differ with him. But there was something going on that they ought to know about. Whereupon he held up a pink sheet of a gossip column called "Whirligig" and read from it. Sent out by the McClure Syndicate, it was not supposed to be printed for public consumption but went to numerous editors. The article said that Roosevelt had been found in a coma at his desk and a significant rash found on the back of his neck. It went on to say he was hustled to the Gulf of Mexico on an alleged fishing trip but in reality had been put aboard a Navy vessel surrounded by guards. Of course, this was a silly statement, because the newspapers and newsreels had shown pictures of his fishing exploits on this trip. Everyone at the press conference laughed at the absurdity of the story.

But there was more dirt. Roosevelt read from a newspaper clipping an excerpt from another McClure confidential column. This clipping quoted an official of the American Cyanamid Company as saying that the greatest danger to this country was that "paranoiac" in the White House; that the best thing that could happen would be for somebody to put two bullets through him. And, if someone would do that, this official would gladly buy him a bottle of champagne to celebrate such an event.

A shudder of horror went through the press conference. Several questions were asked. . . . Was this incitement to crime a violation of law? Could libel action be taken? "No," Roosevelt said, "the President of the United States can do nothing about a thing like this."

A few days later, the National Press Club Board of Governors asked Richard Waldo, President of McClure Syndicate, to appear and show cause why he should not be expelled for insult toward a fellow member—Franklin Roosevelt was an associate member of the club. Waldo appeared and threatened each board member with libel action, declaring that their homes, savings, et cetera, would be seized if he won. The board members naturally hesitated. No formal action ever was taken but Mr. Waldo nevertheless went out of the club.

In late May, 1937, Roosevelt made public his tax evasion story at a press conference. It was substantially as he had outlined to us the night of the Virginia Reel party. There was an amazing reaction in certain newspapers. Editorials and columns said that Roosevelt in attacking the rich tax dodgers was drawing a red herring across the trail. They pooh-poohed his indignation, defended the tax evaders. Instead of indignation against the evaders, indignation was turned back on Roosevelt. Perhaps this was because he had exposed the cynical attacks on his health. Whatever the cause, the strong hatred of him showed that many publishers would spare nothing to attack him.

Reasonable people could find much to criticize in the Roosevelt administration. Some of it was unsound, lots of it showed impetuous errors in judgment. Roy Howard, head of the Scripps-Howard newspapers, believed real opposition to Roosevelt would develop because "The Rooseveltian brand of liberalism is becoming suspect: first, because too much of it is punitive; secondly, too much of it is political almost to the point of demagoguery; and, third, because a lot of it is just plain haywire—impractical and incapable of rendering real benefit or real service to the great masses of the public. . . . Stress is being put on the subject of the division of wealth. Everyone with a grain of sense knows that a complete division of all the wealth earned or created in a single year would make but a slight impression on the annual income of any one citizen. Putting the stress on division, while ignoring the creation of additional wealth, is pure demagoguery."

Ray differed from Mr. Howard. He wrote: "As I understand Roosevelt's program, he is not trying to curtail production at all—except in special crop situations, where exceptional surpluses cause ruinous prices. Fundamentally, he is trying to increase buying power in the lower scale. Most businesses depend upon the mass of people being able to buy things—automobiles, radios, refrigerators. You increase production when they are able to buy and not otherwise. I don't know whether that is division of wealth or not; but, whatever it is, it seems highly desirable for our permanent prosperity and well-being. We'll be years getting the bugs out of all the things Roosevelt has started. The important thing is to make a start. Maybe it isn't perfect, but we can improve it as time goes on. But that is something different from regretting that a start was ever made, or from repudiating Roosevelt because he has failures and makes errors of judgment, like all the rest of us."

As the anti-Roosevelts argued with the pro-Roosevelts, Ray received a letter from a reader saying, "Everybody knows you are frequently entertained at the White House and Roosevelt calls you by your first name. You are a completely prostituted journalist. Your articles show you are blindly, volently and unfairly pro-Roosevelt. At any cost you disclose your hog-tied mentality by poisonous comment. You manufacture news to sustain this prejudice. Roosevelt's food and flattery to you and your wife have rendered you unfit as a political reporter. The public is on to you."

Ray sarcastically answered this letter as follows:

"Ordinarily, I do not answer letters of an insulting nature. But it just happens that last night I was the dinner guest of a former president of the American Bankers' Association and head of one of the largest banks outside of New York City.

I thought you would like to have this information to complete your record of my social life."

As a matter of fact, we were never close to the White House. We were invited only to the regular large receptions, as we had been since President Harding's time, and to a couple of dinners when Ray was president of the Gridiron Club and it was protocol, in a sense, to be invited. Other newspapermen—even Westbrook Pegler—were invited for a week-end to Hyde Park, but never the Clappers. Some people outside of Washington would find this hard to believe. The Roosevelts never tried to seduce Ray with friendship. Ray was not the kind to respond to such treatment if they had. He wanted to be free to criticize or commend either party or any leader. Most newspapermen feel the same way, valuing independence and integrity above everything else.

In the political-economic field all through 1938 and 1939 the same non-cooperation continued between government and business. The unemployed, the ill-housed, ill-fed and ill-clothed were still the unfortunate victims.

The argument of the decade of the nineteen-thirties was the extent to which government should interfere to stimulate business activity. We knew the capitalist system was not self-starting. It needed to have government money pumped into it to keep it going. This was not a new idea. It started away back in our history, when the railroads were subsidized in their earliest days with large grants of land. Otherwise, they could not have expanded across the continent. Farmers had to have many subsidies; manufacturers had to have tariffs; aviation got started by postal subsidies—everybody thought the government should help him.

Another horror people worried themselves sick about was the national debt of 40 billion dollars—doubled in size in a decade. The 69 billions in cash savings of individuals and the 31 billions which national banks had in assets, was also at an all-time high. The government of, by and for the people couldn't go bankrupt as long as all the people had all that cash on hand. We were a big country, with big savings, big capital, and big debts.

Some of the alarmists over the national debt warmed their economics by the old philosophy predicated on the formula that a man should not spend more than he takes in. Neither should the government, they said. Sooner or later, a man who piles up debts that he cannot pay goes bankrupt. It's the same with the government. This debt was getting clear out of sight. How could our grandchildren ever pay it? The government ought to operate like any prudent individual who balances his budget.

This sounds simple and reasonable. Most of us were taught as children to husband every penny and pay cash on the barrel head for things purchased. No debts. Therefore, the government ought to follow the same policy. This is a reasonableness learned at a mother's knee.

The trouble is that it is not that simple. The government is not like one individual—it is a mass of one hundred thirty million people; some, very rich; some, very poor; most, just in-between. To balance the nation's budget, you have to strike a means by which the rich are not taxed too much, yet the poor are not allowed to starve.

While you try to do that with one hand, the other hand is having a dreadful fistfight. With whom? With all of us who demand or need special government help—industry, farmers, labor. We want airfields, schools, post offices, health clinics, subsidies, tariffs. We want economy for every one except ourselves.

Many, many times I have entertained the "Here-to-see-my-Senator" citizens from the South, the North, the East, and the West, who say, "Roosevelt has given away everything—billions of our money." Bitterly they predicted the end of all good life because Roosevelt had given away so much. After they had let off steam about this I always liked to ask: "And why are you in Washington, Mr. Jones? Have you come to urge economy?" Not at all. He had come to get money from Uncle Sam for a new bridge, an airport, or post office for His Town.

Slowly but surely we are learning a bit about our national debt. We are taking a different slant. We are learning that we can balance Uncle Sam's budget if the emphasis is placed in a different spot. That spot is income, not outgo. If sixty million people have steady jobs, our national income will be so big that we'll have to search for many new places to spend it. That's the answer—employment, jobs. Fifty to sixty million jobs could mean one hundred seventy-five billions in the pocketbooks of the nation. Such a vast national income could afford lots of taxes. Taxes pay off the debts. Furthermore, sixty million jobs mean that very few people would be on the relief rolls, further reducing the outgo in government money.

Another thing is that this national debt is owed to ourselves, not to Great Britain, Russia or Uncle Shylock. If we work, stay healthy and produce lots of goods and wealth, we can pay it back—to ourselves. If we cannot provide jobs, we won't have a democracy very long, and we won't have a private capitalistic system either.

True, the capitalistic system wasn't working too well in the thirties. The blight that hit us was world-wide. Other countries were worse off than we were. In over-simplification, we said, "It's that man Roosevelt's fault." Reasonable people knew that any man who was President of the United States in the "dirty thirties" would have been the whipping boy, just as Herbert Hoover was not the cause but the victim of the depression period.

Senator Joseph O'Mahoney of Wyoming, astute, able chairman of a temporary Senate Committee on National Economics, sought to discover why the capitalistic system was not working. He was not satisfied with whimsy. He did not think our system was smashing up because New Dealers were crazy, or because business men were obstinate, or because labor went on sit-down strikes, or because the country had lost confidence in Roosevelt. He marked no one for crucifixion.

He found the difficulty lay deeper than these prejudices. It had to do with an involved, complicated world with a million causes for maladjustment. There was nothing simple about it. For example, at the height of the 1929 boom, you had billions of dollars waiting around, swathed in confidence, ready and willing, all dressed up with no place to go! Big corporations put these idle dollars into the stock market for lack of anything else to do with them. They produced nothing usable except coupon clipping. They didn't build new factories and they put few men to work. Again, ten years later in 1939, we had billions in surplus money lying in bank vaults; we were rich as Croesus but some of our children went barefoot in the snow to school.

The O'Mahoney Committee learned a lot but didn't find the magic formula either. The downward spiral showed 100,000 unemployed in Cleveland. A few bricks went through bakery windows. Men begged for food for their babies. . . .

Suddenly, without fanfare, in the late fall of 1939, something happened. The business cycle turned upward. Barron's business index was 90 percent against 78 percent in 1938. The dividend figures started upward. American initiative started to work. Automobile output jumped 14 percent; freight car loadings rose 11 percent. Du Pont put its marvelous new product made of air, water and coal—the fabulous "Nylon"—on the market, revealing one of the most astounding examples of initiative in a decade.

If the Roosevelt administration had been trying to strike

down American initiative, it had failed dismally. After seven years in office, it was confronted with far more private initiative than had existed when Herbert Hoover resided in the White House. When the New Deal firemen had rushed in, seven years before, to put out the fire that was threatening Uncle Sam's house, they broke up some furniture, which was clumsy of them. But that was about all the damage they did. American initiative survived.

The revival wasn't exactly due to any one's efforts—it just seemed to happen.

Why did we suddenly get going again? Was confidence restored? What secret formula explains it? No one knows. The war orders from abroad accounted for a little of it. But by no means all. The snowball was really rolling again. Industrial production equaled that of 1929. Smoke poured from factory chimneys, machines throbbed, forty-five million people had jobs—happy days were here again.

For some. Nine million were still unemployed after ten years. After all the shouting and cursing, nine million men and women needed and wanted jobs!

Chapter Twelve

SAFE IN THE
WESTERN HEMISPHERE

Abroad, all was chaos as Europe advanced to her Gethsemane. Breathlessly we listened to Hitler's tirades on the radio.

Ray and I had seen and heard Hitler address 40,000 frenzied Germans in Berlin in 1937. We knew something of his fanatical appeal to the German people. Our taxi that night had driven from the Adlon Hotel through miles of soldiers with drawn bayonets on guard along the streets through which Hitler was to pass to the Sportspalast. We passed through tight battalions of guards to enter. The aisles inside the building were lined with still more armed soldiers. Military bands played stirring martial music as only the Germans can play it. We sat in press seats in the balcony very near the stage. All of Nazidom's big shots were there— Goering, Goebbels, Himmler, Hess. The excited audience seethed with heiling and guttural noises. A crimson carpet down the great center aisle threw a red glow upon the faces of Hitler's own elite guard standing shoulder to shoulder in ankle-length black greatcoats and black steel helmets.

Safe in the Western Hemisphere

Every man stood over six feet tall. They resembled giants from Hades with their crimson faces and unsheathed bayonets.

Suddenly a solid roar arose. Everyone was on his feet, men were yelling, women were hysterical. We saw a funny little man in a raincoat run down the aisle and leap upon the platform. He truly resembled Charlie Chaplin to our American eyes. He threw off his hat and coat and leaped upon the stage. He began to speak at once without introduction, as soon as the cheering audience quieted. Words poured from his lips; the famous lock of hair kept falling over his eyes, being pushed back by a jerk of the ever-tossing head; his hands flayed about; mad hysteria filled the air. Thousands listened as one man; the lusty shouts seemed to come from one great mass throat and belly. He raved, he ranted. Were we to be caught in Berlin at the outbreak of war? Surely he was declaring war—nothing short of that could account for the vehemence. I knew little German, so I couldn't follow for an instant this wild rave. I leaned over to an English newspaperman industriously taking notes.

"Please, what is he saying?"

"Oh, he is only telling them to give to the poor."

The occasion was the opening of the winter relief drive—like our Community Chest drives. I sighed gratefully and leaned back to watch Hitler's great act through to the end.

In the two years since that remarkable evening in Berlin we had become convinced that Germany meant to fight another war and that sooner or later the United States would be involved. Lots of other people had the same fear, but there were many more who did not want to believe it and closed their eyes and ears and hearts to the danger.

Sir Wilmot Lewis explained the situation of Great Britain by saying that the dictators were taking turns going through her pockets—two holding her arms while the third took whatever he wanted from her pockets. First, Germany took the Rhineland; then Italy took Ethiopia; then Japan marched into China. With Britain's strength diverted over three fronts and lacking strong allies, what could Britain do but take it lying down?

Then Prime Minister Chamberlain, with his symbolic umbrella, went to meet Adolf Hitler at Munich and, for the sake of peace, sacrificed Czechoslovakia.

I will never forget the dramatic skit that climaxed the Gridiron Club dinner in December, 1938, on the Hitler-Chamberlain pact. The scene was laid in the cabinet room of No. 10 Downing Street, London. At the rear of the room was a large fireplace, over which hung a portrait of Disraeli. Laurel wreaths suggested the Christmas atmosphere. The props were an umbrella, blown inside out, a large red dispatch case, a bunch of roses. The characters included Prime Minister Chamberlain, Lord Halifax—then Foreign Minister—and several Foreign Office secretaries. The secretaries all wore gas masks. They were there to welcome the Prime Minister home from Munich. They were dejected but nonetheless relieved because "our great Prime Minister has been up in the air for 48 hours and is about to come down to earth."

To lessen the tension, one of the secretaries suggested some singing and a good old English song quickly shook the rafters. But then one of the group reminded his colleagues that they would be speaking German soon, and the group took the hint and broke into a German folk song, *Sitz' Ich Allein.*

Into this singular atmosphere rushed Lord Halifax, to announce the arrival of Chamberlain. The roar of airplane propellers was heard. The Prime Minister entered, carrying the umbrella blown inside out, and the secretaries lustily sang out:

> "He is an Englishman!
> For he himself has said it,
> And it's greatly to his credit,
> That he is an Englishman.
> For he might have been a Roosian,
> A French, or Czech or Proosian,
> Or perhaps I-tal-i-an.
> But in spite of all temptations,
> To appease those other nations,
> He remains an Englishman."

Looking as if he had been drawn, indeed, through a knothole, Chamberlain sank wearily into a chair—speechless, dejected, dazed.

There were additional dialogue and other songs, but it was the ending of the skit that had poignant significance.

Safe in the Western Hemisphere

A young secretary who was experiencing his first visit to No. 10 Downing Street asked a question that stilled all merriment. "Whose picture is that hanging over the fireplace?" he wanted to know. The room grew deathly quiet as Halifax replied:

"That, sir, is the portrait of a man who was once Prime Minister of England—perhaps the greatest Prime Minister Britain ever had. His name was Disraeli. He was—a Jew!"

And then, as the light grew dim, and the group was reminded of the nearness of Christmas, the Gridiron Club did something it never had done before. It ended a skit—and its dinner—with a hymn:

"Away in a manger, no crib for his bed,
The little Lord Jesus lay down His sweet head;
The stars in the sky looked down where He lay,
The little Lord Jesus, asleep in the hay."

Peace was what we wanted, but would we get it? Europe was up to its old tricks of bloodletting. They were not going to get us into their infernal troubles again! We were safe in the Western Hemisphere, between the Atlantic and the Pacific. We would stay home and mind our own business. . . .

To make sure that we were insulated against Europe's fratricides, we had a law which we hoped would keep us out of the fray. It was called the Neutrality Act. It contained an embargo against the sale of arms to belligerent nations; it provided that no American vessel could carry arms, ammunition or implements of war to or for any belligerent; that no American vessel trading in other goods with a belligerent could be armed; that no American citizen could travel on any ship of a belligerent. The purpose of these provisions was to minimize the chances of loss of American lives and property, which might involve this country in trouble with belligerents. The Neutrality Act had to be invoked by a Presidential Proclamation, designating the countries at war as belligerents.

We tried to legislate protection for ourselves, based on experiences in other wars; but the war that was coming up was a different kind of a war. The unknown quantity in it was the use of air power. We didn't realize to what an extent airplanes, superfortresses, robot bombs, could jump over fortifications and oceans. We had yet to learn that air power could destroy sea power.

We forgot something else in our frantic desire to isolate ourselves—our dependence upon the British Navy. For one hundred and fifty years, since the infancy of the United States, we had been unafraid of foreign foes because the British Navy operated to our advantage. With the oceans in friendly hands, we could expand across a continent without a backward glance for enemies on our frontiers.

It was, therefore, greatly to our national interest that the status quo of naval power be preserved. It gave us a world more to our advantage if we had a strong community of interest with Great Britain, despite the fact that we were trade rivals. We soon began to realize that it would be almost a fatal day for us if that sea power was broken.

So long as the British maintained their strength in the Far East, we had no serious worry about the safety of our supply of rubber, tin, and hemp. We could not feel so secure about these supplies if Japan rather than Britain held Singapore. The vision of a Tokyo-Rome-Berlin combination attacking the Western Hemisphere was menacing.

The British played the game according to the same rules we used. Germany did not. She was a trade threat, not yet a military threat. At first, Germany and other totalitarian countries were rapidly stepping up their challenge to our markets in the Western Hemisphere. Old-fashioned methods of individual trading had been scrapped. Our idea was that an American maker of harmonicas, for instance, gathers up his supply, goes down to Rio and looks for customers. He makes his deals just as he did at home. That wasn't the way Germany operated. All her trading was controlled, managed, and operated to meet specific national needs. What she bought and sold depended not upon what her business men happened to want to sell or buy, but upon what her government, from the viewpoint of its whole economy, wanted to buy and sell. She went to any lengths—subsidizing, bartering, using squeeze plays of all sorts, up to and including boycott threats—anything that seemed effective to get what she needed.

There was another factor in the Nazi regime that we did not like. That was the outrages perpetrated against the Jews.

Safe in the Western Hemisphere

Friends returning from Germany told us that the population stood silent and fearful at the Nazis' brutalities to the Jews. The streets were jammed with people who were afraid to say a word lest they get into trouble. Young Nazis not only beat up or killed Jews, they broke into Jewish-owned shops, came out with armfuls of goods, which they then peddled for their own pockets. The anti-Semitic fever had its repercussions in this country. Frequently it took the form of the question: Are we going to fight a war to save the Jews in Germany?

As we slowly sensed the oncoming storm, Hitler kept the situation confused and worried. Bloodlessly he continued to annex territory. I remember someone cleverly said that Chamberlain took his week-ends in the country, whereas Hitler took his countries in the week-end. He wanted Danzig, he wanted a path across the Polish Corridor, he wanted colonies. Time and again, he pledged that he did not want anything, but he continued to scorn such pledges week after week. He developed the technique of destroying weak governments from within. It soon became clear that an encircling movement of awesome proportions was going on.

Japan crowded the British in the Far East; Italy menaced the Mediterranean life line. Germany expanded into the Baltic.

This changing balance of world power concerned the United States. We could faintly sense that Hitler's overseas imperialism was bound to collide with us sooner or later— particularly as Japan was likely to be in combination with him. Painfully, slowly, the fact emerged that our national interests demanded that we give the breaks to England and France—even if we were charged with non-neutrality. Gradually our policy developed into a desire to give aid to the democracies, short of war. The fixed and imperative first principle was to protect the Western Hemisphere, subject to no qualifications. Secondly, it was a better world for us with the British patrolling the rest of the world. The question then arose: How much is this advantage worth? We began to see that it was easily worth materials, airplanes, foodstuffs, to Britain and France.

Of course, a lot of people didn't agree with this change in foreign policy. They recalled that George Washington in his farewell address said that we should steer clear of entangling alliances. What Washington actually said in his farewell address was that we should steer clear of permanent alliances; but this argument didn't carry much weight, because history clearly showed that George Washington took a practical view of conditions in his own period. No doubt this practical statesman of old would have seen that the United States was caught in a position where she could not be neutral. Our vast economic resources exerted a decisive effect upon the relative strength of the opposing powers. If we refused our resources to all the belligerents, it would help Germany, because she had more resources at her disposal than did Britain and France. If we sold supplies to Britain and France who, since they controlled the seas, were the only belligerents in a position to come and get the supplies, we were not neutral. For us, neutrality could be only a state of mind—nothing more. No matter what we did, we exerted an effect beyond computation. Only the small, inconsequential nations could be neutral. We were the victims of our enormous resources, for they exerted their force in world politics, whether we wanted them to or not! We were helpless in the matter.

We were not helpless, however, to say where this force should be directed. If we failed to direct it anywhere, it was automatically directed in favor of Germany.

President Roosevelt did not look at the European situation in terms of aloofness. He was in daily communication by telephone with Ambassador Kennedy in London and Ambassador Bullitt in Paris. The hourly moves in the tense European situation were brought close to Roosevelt's desk. Working in such an atmosphere, he had a sense of intimate association with events in Europe. He made a peace proposal in April, 1939, in the hope of prolonging discussion to postpone the day of actual fighting. He warned Hitler and Mussolini that the tremendous force of the United States must be a factor in their thinking; that the United States was far from indifferent to their plottings; that a war forced by them would from the outset involve the destinies of a nation which they should realize was potentially far stronger than Germany and Italy united.

He tried a little to undermine public sentiment in Germany and Italy in the same way that Woodrow Wilson sought to undermine the German people's faith in the Kaiser in World War I. Wilson made successful use of such propaganda behind the German and Austrian lines. In speeches, Wilson reiterated that there was no war against the German people but only against their autocratic rulers. However, in 1939 not much confidence could be placed in such technique, because it was impossible to get through to the peoples behind Hitler and Mussolini. With the controlled press and radio, nothing reached the people against the wishes of their leaders.

But there was a more basic reason than this why the people were not eager to turn against these rulers. The average German felt that Hitler was winning the whole continent of Europe without losing a soldier. Everybody was at work in Germany and Italy. They had a sense of accomplishment and of progress toward the fulfillment of a larger destiny. In contrast, the picture which they were given of democratic countries was one of unemployment and depression, futility and internal bickering, and fumbling indecision in face of the compact, aggressive march of their own dictators.

The oncoming fight was not only a struggle between dictatorships and democracies. It was a struggle over power. Nations were moved by cold national interests. Power is more important than ideology. Each country was gravitating in the direction to which its national interests drew it. We began to see that the only standard upon which we could realistically base our policy was that of the national interests of the United States, rather than any sentimentality about democracy. We had the Western Hemisphere to protect.

Safe in the Western Hemisphere

We had to keep our access to rubber and tin in the East Indies. British sea power was more comfortable for us than Japanese and German sea power.

Our Secretary of State, Cordell Hull, clearly had the solution of the problem of trade for the world. He was a free trader. He saw menace to world economy in rising tariffs, restrictions, and artificial barriers erected to stand in the way of a free flow of goods among the nations. He saw that these things meant slow strangulation of world trade and a consequent reduction of national income. He set about with the single-minded persistence which dominated him to abolish these evil barriers.

He conceived of trade as an operation that ought to bring profit to both parties. He tried to bring this about by negotiations with other nations, because we couldn't let down our barriers unless other nations did likewise. We proposed to give equal treatment with all other nations which gave us equal treatment. This was called "reciprocal trade agreements."

It was a long, hard, slow process. It required negotiation over commodity after commodity with each nation interested. Yet, in nine years, he had succeeded in making agreements with some 20 countries, which represented 60 percent of our total imports and 57 percent of our exports. It was a remarkable success. Given a reasonable orderly world, Hull's arrangements might have produced the long-range answer to world peace and recovery; but he was not given that orderly world.

Safe in the Western Hemisphere

While the great debate about Europe proceeded, we likewise ducked and squirmed and looked away from a problem
that was very close to us. Were we going to stay in the Far
East? Were we going to hold the Philippines, or were we
ready to see Japan take complete control in the Western
Pacific? She had captured the last important Chinese seaport
and controlled the whole Chinese coast. British citizens were
humiliated and subjected to personal indignities. Japan had
about decided to throw the Occidental out of the Orient.

When Roosevelt came into the Presidency, he had privately expressed concern over the attitude of Japan, saying,
"Japan is now ruled by a lot of lieutenant colonels. The
military party is in the ascendency, and a liberal statesman
runs a good chance of assassination." He worried because the
defense plans of the United States for the Philippines were
much the same as they were at the end of 1920, when he
left the Navy Department.

At that time the Orange Plan, drawn up by the General
Staff of the Army, called for immediate withdrawal of all
ships of war stationed in the islands, should hostilities open
up between this nation and Japan. Military experts were
convinced that with our inadequate equipment in the Philippines they could not be defended against invasion by a force
as strong as Japan had. Soldiers on the islands would have
to be left to their fate. Roosevelt lived to see these predictions come true.

The cold situation which faced us now had two alterna-
tives. We could green-light Japan's determination to domi-

nate the Orient as we dominated the Western Hemisphere, which meant that in time we would have to obtain rubber for our automobile industry and tin for industrial purposes at the pleasure of Japan. It meant that we would sell goods in Eastern Asia subject to Japanese conditions. It meant that we would have to get out of the Philippines.

To take that course, we needed immediately to put our economic affairs in shape for a drastic readjustment. The rubber industry would have to be developed, both synthetically and by the planting of young rubber trees in the Western Hemisphere. Tin substitutes would have to be devised. Our Navy would have to be pulled back to Pearl Harbor, to form a rim around the Western Hemisphere.

The second alternative was to make a stand at once, apply the strongest threats of pressure to Japan—such as cutting off cotton, a severe blow to our own Southland; cutting off munitions and industrial exports to Japan, a blow to our industry in the North; and getting our Navy in a position to meet any retaliation that might result from such a course.

We took neither of these stands but drifted, waited, and hoped for the best. We had yet to learn that we were living in a dangerous world. The power of decision was to be taken out of our hands.

Secretary Hull's record in the Far Eastern situation was clear for all to read. I remember conferences which he had from time to time with my husband, during which he reiterated over and over again that Japan was determined to dominate Eastern Asia, the Russia coast, China and the Pacific

Islands. Few believed Hull, but he knew what the real score was.

His strategy was to keep Tokyo and Berlin guessing, making no definite commitments of policy. It angered him always when any Congressman got up and said that we would not send a single man to fight in Europe, because that weakened us with the Fascist powers. He felt that it was urgent to repeal the arms embargo, because if we let it stand on our books it encouraged Hitler and Tojo.

Then all of a sudden Fascism and Communism embraced to break the power of democracy in Europe. The Nazis signed a non-aggression pact with Russia. With the stroke of a pen, the balance of power shifted decisively. Dictatorship advanced day by day and democracy retreated. Maps began to show huge, dominant, black areas of dictatorship.

The future was put on an hour-to-hour basis. The way of life which had been slanted for some centuries in the direction of self-government and individual freedom seemed destined for extinction. Suddenly we saw that Hitler had forged a state which was more effective than democracy. Suddenly it was questionable whether Britain could survive without also becoming a dictatorship. France, in the emergency, had already become one. Was the hand on the clock swinging westward to the United States?

And then it came. . . . WAR! War over Poland. War between Germany and the Allies—France and Great Britain. We had been fearing it for such a long time that when it actually came it carried a doubled shock.

Safe in the Western Hemisphere

I remember that our family was going down to the beach for a quiet day. We made an early start and stopped at a "Hot Shoppe" for breakfast before driving on to the beach. It was hard to believe the black headlines. When we got down to the quiet cottage on the seashore, marching armies seemed very far away and unimportant as the sun sparkled on the blue water. As we drove back to Washington that night, the news came that the *Athenia,* an English vessel filled with women and children, had been sunk off the coast of England. The twenty years between the two wars seemed non-existent. I could remember the sinking of the *Lusitania.* We were right back where we had started; the world had learned nothing.

A few nights later, I sat at a dinner with a group of housing experts to discuss a program for building houses for farm laborers in Maryland. During dinner, everyone was discussing our neutrality, insisting that this time we certainly would remember the lessons of the past and stay on our own side of the Atlantic Ocean. I was seated beside the architect who would plan the comfortable little homes to be built in Maryland. He was a German. He spoke with a marked accent. He was tall, robust, and blond—the kind of German Hitler particularly idealized. I tried to talk about trivial matters, but we could not disregard the loud unanimity of the other guests, who were insisting that the European war was none of our affair. Suddenly, to my astonishment, the German leaped to his feet and in dramatic tones said approximately the following:

Safe in the Western Hemisphere

"I was born in Germany. I fought in the Kaiser's army in the last war as a very young man. After the war I went back to Berlin and was immediately put to work designing air bases. There was never a minute when we considered anything but the next war—in which Germany would be triumphant. I did not like to contemplate another war. I went to Russia in my search for a system of government under which I thought I could live my life in peace. I did not find it in Russia. Next I came to the United States . . . only lately have I become a citizen. Perhaps I have no right to speak to you, but I hear you talking that this war is none of your business. I tell you, it is! I know of plans in the War Ministry in Berlin, which call for an invasion of the Western Hemisphere. I tell you that the final battle of this war will be fought on the shores of Nova Scotia; locked in mortal combat in that battle will be the army of the United States fighting German troops—brought over on British warships long since captured from a defeated Britain!"

With tears streaming down his face, he sat down muttering, "You say it's none of your business!"

My husband, along with millions of others, felt for a long time that we could stay out of the war if we really wanted to. History records conquests throughout the centuries. Great Britain had built her enormous empire by conquest and snatched strategic outposts and areas for trade. She had seized India, taken South Africa, grabbed part of the Dutch possessions in the east, established footholds in China, and a strategic base in the Mediterranean. France had done similarly well for herself. While we admitted a preference for the old style of war lords and conquering nations to the stark, horrible efficiency of the new ones, we had nevertheless concentrated our energies on making our way of life in the Western Hemisphere an impregnable stronghold.

The President issued a Proclamation of Limited Emergency—again showing his astute psychology. He could have done all the things he needed to do at the moment without issuing the proclamation; but he did this so that his next step would not be such a shock, when full emergency became necessary. It was a conditioning of our people. . . . It helped to impress the American people with the seriousness of the situation; and it showed governments abroad that we were not asleep on the job and would help to forestall sabotage and spy organizations such as were set up in the first war.

Frank Murphy, pleasant, sincere and conscientious Attorney General at that time, told Ray that he thought it was an eight-to-one chance that the Allies would be licked. He recalled that Germany almost won alone last time and that now she had Russia and Italy, both of whom might be on her side this time. Since the chances were so much against British-French victory, he thought we must be prepared, that we must expect and get ready for anything.

Very soon the world became conscious that two new weapons of unanticipated power and skill would probably determine the outcome of this war—the bombing plane and the submarine. Germany dispatched these weapons in increasing numbers all over the Atlantic. Within the securest fleet bases, submarines and airplanes destroyed units of the British fleet. We sensed that this method of warfare was as revolutionary as the use of gunpowder.

With renewed interest, we looked to our own defenses. What we saw was not encouraging. We had appropriated enough money to dredge the harbor of Guam, but we opposed any fortification of it. We had no Army at all and very little air power.

As we danced out the old year, 1939, and the New Year in, somber forebodings disturbed our gayest moments. What would happen in 1940? What did the seeming stalemate in Europe's phony war mean? What of our own beloved country? Would Roosevelt be nominated for a third term? Did the Republicans have anyone who could beat him? Could nothing be done to bring us unity on the tottering brink?

For us as Americans it had been a good life. Our golden days were to slip inevitably from us. We would say good-bye soon to the land we had known. Lingering on the brink, we tasted the past fondly, like lovers about to be parted forever. We had had our troubles, but tomorrow was always full of promise. Whether we went to war or not, we would act more and more as if we were. Our ways would change drastically; peace-times would be sacrificed.

We had had a grand life in America. We had had to work hard. But, usually, there was good reward. We had had poverty, but every individual had the hope that if he threw his best into the struggle he could gain security and dignity. In every one of us, there lived the promise of America; under every man's foot, the firm security of a nation strong, good and safe.

The distant fire was rolling toward us. The evil wind blew. The dear days were dying. . . .

Chapter Thirteen

A SINGER,
A SERIOUS MAN,
A STANDARD BEARER

As Hitler tortured and murdered the Jews and gobbled up one small country after another, we experienced in Washington a mixture of red tape and prejudice which kept the great Negro contralto, Marian Anderson, from the concert stage in this capital of democracy. She wasn't allowed to sing in the D.A.R. Hall or in the public school auditoriums, but she did sing at the foot of the noble statue of the Emancipator of her race—on the steps of the Lincoln Memorial.

The idea of having Marian Anderson sing on the steps of the Lincoln Memorial originated in the mind of that noble human being, the Assistant Secretary of the Interior, Oscar Chapman. His idea grew out of an incident in his childhood. He was born in Virginia and as a lad in grade school had had a stern lesson in intolerance. He was in the eighth-grade graduating class. The pupils took up a collection to buy a present for their school. Oscar was delegated by his schoolmates to buy the gift. He bought a picture of Lincoln.

Although Oscar was a Virginian by birth, the ideals and humanness of Abraham Lincoln fired his natural instincts. The picture was hung in the schoolroom, but his classmates carried word home to their parents, who cried out in anger that a picture of the Civil War President should be hung in the school. The school board was enraged and the picture was ordered taken down. Oscar was suspended from school. A Methodist Sunday School superintendent interceded, however, and Oscar was restored to his class. Oscar rehung the picture of Lincoln and, when ordered to take it down again, refused. Bewildered by the angry feelings aroused in the school board, Oscar began to ask questions and has continued asking them all of his life. He has taken the side of tolerance every time that opportunity has come his way.

The committee handling the arrangements for Marian Anderson's appearance to sing on the steps of the Lincoln Memorial was headed by Secretary of the Interior Ickes. I was asked to serve on the Citizens' Committee. On Friday, before the Easter Sunday concert, I received a call from the committee asking if I could arrange a place where Marian Anderson might be allowed to rest for a couple of hours before her concert. She was arriving in Washington at 1 P.M.; the concert was at 5 P.M. No hotel in the capital of this nation, dedicated to the principle that "all men are created equal," would accept a reservation for this distinguished artist, whose voice Arturo Toscanini said was one "heard only once in a hundred years."

Could I find a place where she might rest before her concert? Of course I could! I called Mrs. Gifford Pinchot, wife of the former Governor of Pennsylvania, always a fighter for progress, whose town house was conveniently located in the center of town and whose doors were always open to the oppressed. Of course, she would be honored to have Marian Anderson at her house but, unfortunately, she would have to be absent at a luncheon for a couple of hours and could not be there to greet Miss Anderson upon her arrival. Could I take her place as hostess until 3 P.M.?

The next couple of days were filled with rumors and forebodings and threats against Marian Anderson. I was assured that sufficient police protection would be thrown about the Pinchot house, in case any attempt was made to annoy her.

My daughter, Janet, was just sixteen and already an ardent believer in tolerance for all human beings. She was greatly aroused over the threats. As I left my home to go to the Pinchot residence to welcome Miss Anderson, Janet said, "Mother, if Miss Anderson is worried or frightened, promise me that you will tell her not to be frightened, but to relax and let her glorious voice roll out to us in all its beauty."

Of course, I had no idea of mentioning this message to Miss Anderson, but when she arrived at Mrs. Pinchot's she was obviously shaken and frightened. When, in greeting, I asked, "How are you?" she said, "Oh, Mrs. Clapper, I have never been so frightened in all my life! I don't see how I can possibly sing."

Remembering Janet's admonition, I placed both my hands on her arm and said, "I have a message for you from my young daughter." And I repeated Janet's words. Tears slowly formed in Miss Anderson's eyes and silently dropped down her cheeks as she said, "Thank you very much. That was all I needed. I will be all right now."

She rested until 4:30, when she came out dressed for her concert in a crimson blouse and black velvet skirt. Miss Anderson is a large woman with regal bearing. She looked like a massive dark-skinned goddess. Her mother—in contrast—was a tiny little woman, born of poverty, who had scrubbed and worked all of her life to insure the training of her daughter's voice. Miss Anderson's manager handed her mother a small orchid to be pinned on Marian's shoulder. It was about as effective as a sweet pea. When Miss Anderson, conscious of how silly the little orchid looked on her, tried to pin it on her mother instead, a slight controversy arose between the manager and Miss Anderson about who should wear the orchid. The manager momentarily won the argument, but I was amused to note as we got out of the motor cars at the Lincoln Memorial that Mama Anderson was wearing the orchid.

We took our seats on the platform, and Miss Anderson went to a waiting room in the interior. No words could ever describe the beauty and meaning of the great scene that stretched before our eyes. From behind the great marble pillars of the memorial, the massive, seated, sculptured figure of Abraham Lincoln looked down across a multitude of black-and-white humanity stretching as far as the eye could see, past the Mirror Pool and on to the Washington Monument far to the east. This outdoor audience of 75,000 people gathered like waves of the sea and stood waiting to witness a great triumph. Marian Anderson's entrance, carrying a sheaf of enormous American Beauty roses, was simple and very dramatic as she came slowly down the marble steps on the arm of Harold Ickes. He introduced her by saying:

"In this great auditorium under the sky, all of us are free. When God gave us this wonderful outdoors and the sun and the moon and the stars, He made no distinction of race or creed or color; and 130 years ago, He sent to us one of His truly great . . . Abraham Lincoln. . . . Today we stand reverently and humbly at the base of this memorial to the Great Emancipator, while glorious tribute is rendered to his memory by a daughter of the race from which he struck the chains of slavery. . . . Genius, like Justice, is blind. For Genius has touched with the tip of her wing this woman. . . . Genius draws no color line."

Marian Anderson took her place and, gloriously vibrant, sang *America*. She sang with her eyes closed—effortlessly and without gestures, and enchantment settled over the vast crowds. The setting sun bathed the reflection pool, and no eye was dry as she intoned the crescendo of Schubert's *Ave Maria* with a splendor which no other artist in the world could match. So overwhelming was the beauty that applause was an intrusion. When the haunting melodies of simple, religious, Negro spirituals filled the air, the listeners were transfigured with a new conception of the meaning of Easter.

As the political picture opened up in 1940, strange shadows flickered on the walls, and the American spirit was heavy with uncertainty. Questions that affected Republicans and Democrats alike were deep, often unasked. Would the war break loose with real hell-fury in the spring? What would that be like? What about the Russians? Would the British be able to weather the attack in the spring? If not, how much would we care? Could our vexing domestic problems ever be settled?

Everyone in Washington was trying to dope out whether, when the Democrats convened in Chicago, the President would announce plans for a third term. Paraphrasing Confucius, someone said, "When convention meet in windy city, look out for draft."

The extent of the effort to find out President Roosevelt's third-term intentions was indicated at a meeting of the Defense Commission one day, when the President announced that he was calling a joint meeting of the Cabinet and the Commission on a certain day. Leon Henderson spoke up to say he wouldn't be able to come because he would be out of town.

"Where are you going?" asked the President.

"To a meeting of the Shouting Club in Chicago—you remember? You and I joined it in 1932. I've paid my dues," Leon smilingly said. "Have you?"

"Yes," laughed Roosevelt, "I've paid my dues."

"Well, then," angled Leon, "aren't you going out to the reunion, Mr. President?"

"You will go out to Chicago," said Roosevelt, "and you will fish, Leon, but you won't catch any more fish out there than you will by the fishing you are doing right now."

Leon Henderson, the chief New Dealer on the Defense Commission, won great respect among business men engaged in the defense effort. At first, they had been skeptical of him, and regarded him as a spy from the New Deal camp, to be treated with suspicion. But Henderson proved one of the toughest and most realistic men on the Commission, and puzzled many of his old New Deal cronies by his impatience with their talk of "preserving social gains." He had not lost his enthusiasm for social gains, but he regarded defense production as the nation's first requirement, calling for sacrifice all around, including sacrifice by labor.

Henderson was the best debater in the Defense Commission, but he is said to have met his match in William Knudsen. Henderson tried to convince Knudsen on a detail of the defense program. Knudsen listened to Henderson patiently. When the argument was completed, Knudsen said, "No, Leon, we won't do that." That settled it. Henderson didn't know how to handle a fellow who wouldn't argue back.

The polls of public opinion in 1940 reported gigantic popular majorities for President Roosevelt, preferring him for a third term to most of the other candidates combined. Yet on a trip across the country, my husband found no insistent demand that the President run. In fact, he found little popular enthusiasm for any of the presidential personalities in either party.

Thomas E. Dewey came the nearest to a real glamor personality in the field. Yet the distinct feeling was that he was a boy up for a man's job. Newspaperman James Lloyd Wright said that Dewey impressed him "as being intolerant of mediocrity in a country where there is a lot of that." Dewey was a man of very rare mental ability, but the trouble was, he knew it himself. He lacked the guile to appear less mentally superior than he really was. Nobody knew very much about Mr. Dewey's policies, or whether he had any deeply rooted convictions. He was against defeatism and endorsed optimism. Ken Simpson said that Dewey offered "hope and an expansion of credit." But Ray answered that it looked to him as though Dewey stood for "faith, hope and damn little charity."

My husband had had a little experience with Mr. Dewey, growing out of the bitter feud between Kenneth Simpson and Thomas Dewey in New York State politics.

Kenneth Simpson, young, aggressive, intelligent Republican Liberal, had coached Dewey, leading him into a liberalism of promise. In 1937 and 1938, many people hoped that this leadership might overthrow the Tories in the Republican Party. But Simpson and Dewey broke off their relationship and Dewey tended to lean more and more toward a conservative policy.

Because this inter-party fight in New York State was of national interest, my husband interviewed Kenneth Simpson and Thomas Dewey repeatedly and wrote articles about it. At first he lauded Dewey for his apparent liberalism and then bemoaned the break-up with Simpson. The key to Dewey's success, my husband felt, was in the continued influence of Kenneth Simpson.

Thomas Dewey repeatedly told my husband the details of his and Simpson's disagreement. Yet in an interview on June 29, 1939, Dewey calmly and coldly said, "There has never been any situation between us. You wrote a lot of fiction in those articles." That set my husband back on his heels. Dumbfounded, he said, "You told me a good deal of that, yourself." Dewey denied that, and Ray asked that he have his secretary bring in copies of his columns and point out to him the parts of the articles that were not true.

Ray said, "You told me yourself that Simpson was a millstone around your neck and you had to get rid of him; that you would see to it that he was thrown out of office as County Chairman of the Republican Party." That stopped Dewey, and he began to argue about small details. According to accurate notes written in my husband's diary around April 1, 1939, Dewey had said Simpson was a paranoiac and that he had shown, even as a college man at Yale, that he couldn't be depended upon.

Soon Dewey's secretary brought the articles about which

Dewey was complaining into the room, and Dewey pointed to a statement in one which said that Simpson had made Dewey the District Attorney.

Dewey said, "That burns me up. . . . I'm not anybody's stooge."

Ray answered, "That wasn't what I was saying in the article. You told me yourself that Simpson dragged you in as a candidate for District Attorney. Last April you blamed Simpson for it. Now you quibble about it."

Dewey accused Ray of being hostile to him, although a few months previously, when Ray had written some favorable pieces, Dewey had been beside himself with appreciation and warmth.

Ray said, "That's the way it is with a columnist. I wrote yards of favorable copy about you; yet now, because there is something in these last articles you don't like, you say I am hostile. I am only trying to picture the situation as it looks."

Ray was shocked at Dewey's cold-blooded shift of position, blandly ignoring the fiery hatred he had expressed for Ken Simpson only three months before when he had even gone to the lengths of specifically asking Ray not to seat Simpson next to him at the Gridiron dinner.

The conversation continued with more discussion of the New York political situation and also some national issues, particularly, agricultural problems. They parted in good humor; but Ray noted in his diary that Dewey showed great imperiousness and a disposition to pay little attention to what he had said before. He could hardly have failed to recall the amazing things he had told Ray about Simpson. His bland passing them off as trivialities and his complete misrepresentation of some other details showed faulty memory or sharp distortion. In his diary Ray wrote:

"I suspect Dewey is a victim of intense emotions which are so powerful that they overwhelm his recollection and distort it to the purposes of the moment. To my mind, Dewey appears to be swelling rather than growing."

Unsuccessful in 1940, Thomas Dewey did win the Republican nomination in 1944 in Chicago. Speaking over the radio immediately following his acceptance speech, I, as a radio reporter, described the beautiful Mrs. Thomas Dewey. In the course of my remarks I said that the Governor was in the habit of reading his speeches to his wife, and that undoubtedly, like other wives, she made suggestions and perhaps at times she even criticized. It seemed a very innocuous bit of chatter, which Mrs. Dewey herself confirmed the next day at her press conference.

Early the next morning, I was awakened by a Western Union messenger thrusting a telegram at me, signed by an unknown man in Los Angeles, as follows:

"YOUR SUGGESTION ON THE AIR, LAST NIGHT, THAT GOVERNOR DEWEY CONSULTS HIS WIFE HAS DONE IRREPARABLE DAMAGE TO GOVERNOR DEWEY AND THE REPUBLICAN PARTY. WHY DON'T YOU DO WHAT THE GENERAL PUBLIC WISHES MRS. ROOSEVELT WOULD DO—GO SIT ON A TACK AND SHUT UP."

A Singer, a Serious Man, a Standard Bearer

It was just one of those little tidbits with which the American public loves to shower its commentators.

In August I was commissioned by *Look* magazine to write a piece about Mrs. Dewey, her interests and her activities. I went up to Albany on a hot, sticky day, enjoying the cool ride along the beautiful Hudson River. Both the Governor and Mrs. Dewey received me cordially.

There were seven of us at luncheon that day: the Governor and Mrs. Dewey, eleven-year-old Tommie Dewey and his younger brother, Mrs. Irene Kuhn, who was handling Mrs. Dewey's publicity, the Governor's secretary, and myself. When the dessert came in, the boys were having watermelon but the adults had delicious French pancakes. The watermelon, cut into old-fashioned, generous slices, was brought in on plates that were a little small. In his eagerness to gobble up the watermelon, Tommie thrust his fork into the delicious, red heart, but it slipped off the fork, skidded across the highly polished table in front of me, to fall ignominiously upon the floor.

Governor Dewey shouted in thunderous tones: "Tommie, if you don't know how to eat watermelon, get up and leave the table!"

Tommie flushed and tears came into his eyes. We were all very embarrassed. I started to murmur in his defense that it didn't matter, that any boy eating watermelon was apt to have a similar accident. But before speaking I remembered that I was there to write a story about Mrs. Dewey, and this was a family crisis, to which I should note Mrs. Dewey's reaction. I know if it had happened at my own table, I would have risen to the defense of the child. Mrs. Dewey did not. She backed up her husband's discipline effectively, saying, "Tommie, your father is right."

It was a little incident of no consequence, but as I sat there thinking of the multitudinous, fatiguing pullings and haulings to which the President of the United States is subjected, I couldn't picture Mr. Dewey maintaining a presidential poise, if, in such a small matter as this, he allowed his temper to overcome him completely.

Back in 1940 the Republicans had two other candidates for the Republican nomination—Senator Vandenberg, who struck a pose of magnificent disinterest, and Senator Taft, who put on an old-style, well-heeled drive for delegates. Neither aroused any great popular interest. If Senator Robert Taft had had the personality of his brilliant wife, Martha, he would have been a formidable candidate.

One young Republican who was making a brilliant record at this time was Harold Stassen, Governor of Minnesota. I shared my husband's enthusiasm for this young man who combined intelligence with a progressive outlook and common sense. In a state torn by labor battles, with extreme feelings on both sides, he had put through mediation legislation that steered a moderate course between the extremes of radical Laborites and the Republican Tories who, if they had had their way in Minnesota, would have gone back to black-listing and yellow-dog contracts. Given a man of such broad intelligence, common sense and courage, you never have to worry very much about his philosophy of government because such a man will in the long run strike a balance which is to the benefit of the public. We were glad to see Harold Stassen becoming seasoned for national service. Our friendship which has grown with the years is strengthened by our mutual efforts for a world security plan. As long as our country produces men of Stassen's calibre, democracy will flourish.

As the Republican Convention convened the ablest Republican member of the House, Representative Joseph Martin, was made permanent chairman. Throughout the past ten years, this competent parliamentarian held the confidence and leadership of his minority party members. He made the Republicans something more than a handful of bellowing critics, and mobilized them into a compact, hard-hitting opposition. In less arduous times, his pedestrian vision might have made him good material for the presidential candidacy.

As the Republican campaign picture came into focus, all these candidates were subject to a mysterious process that obeys no formula. American politics has curious ways. For example, Coolidge and Franklin D. Roosevelt achieved success although they had nothing in common, either in personality or methods. Franklin D. Roosevelt, probably the greatest politician we have ever had, failed to eliminate the unemployment which he inherited from the repudiated Hoover, but he remained highly popular in spite of that failure.

Neither party put on a convention during this campaign

in which democracy could take any pride. In Philadelphia, the Republicans were infuriated when two of their illustrious members, Colonel Frank Knox and Henry L. Stimson, accepted Cabinet positions in the Roosevelt Government because of the war crisis. The Republicans practically branded them as traitors to the party.

The strong anti-war delegations at the Republican Convention tried to picture Roosevelt as taking the country into war. One Congressman said that Mr. Roosevelt's proposed transfer of over-age destroyers to Great Britain was a felony, for which the President ought to be imprisoned; another declared that Mr. Roosevelt was taking us into war, shouting, "We ain't mad at nobody." Still another delegate said, "The people in this country are not afraid of Hitler; they are afraid of Roosevelt."

There were political scavengers seeking votes in any way they could get them and paying little heed to the responsible national leaders of the Republican Party, who did not want to put a millstone around the neck of an Administration dealing with critical situations arising out of the war developments.

In passing, it is important to note that the same Republican reactionary financiers controlled the party as in 1936, and as they were destined to do in 1944. These were hard-bitten, tough foes of New Deal reform such as Ernest T. Weir and Joe Pew. Ernest Weir bawled out Senator Arthur Vandenberg for an article in the January, 1940, issue of the *American Mercury*, in which Vandenberg tried to set forth a progressive attitude for his party. Weir was raising the money for the campaign and he was going to call the time. He and his fellow millionaires of rugged individualism cried their salty tears over the naughty New Deal on the polished decks of their yachts.

The men who financed the Republican Party during the twelve years of Roosevelt's era were incapable for the most part of seeing the conditions that were changing the world's structure. Time and again, they missed the boat, and in the campaign of 1940 their hatred of their nominee Wendell Willkie was second only to their hatred of Roosevelt.

Mr. Dewey did not get the nomination in Philadelphia, nor did Senator Taft, or Senator Vandenberg. By one of the strangest freaks of politics in this country, Wendell Willkie was nominated out of an overwhelming cry for leadership from the people themselves, as opposed to the politicians. The people saved the Republican politicians from themselves. Out of their determination that democracy should not fall victim to the creeping paralysis abroad, out of a yearning for intelligence, energy, and courage, they forced a big man to the leadership of the party.

I first met both Thomas Dewey and Wendell Willkie the same night at a reception Eleanor Patterson, publisher of the Washington *Times-Herald,* gave after the spring Gridiron dinner in 1940, about three months before the Republican Convention. As soon as Dewey walked into the huge second-floor hall, a group collected around him. He had assurance, a certain pompous gayety. His brown eyes had a way of boring into yours. I joined the group and listened. Obviously he was a candidate. I had heard that he worked very hard on his campaign speeches; sometimes thirty hours of labor went into a thirty-minute speech. Someone, I also recalled, wisecracked that Dewey had learned a lot about national affairs by reading the campaign speeches which his braintrust wrote for him.

My attention wandered across to the corner where a man, whose face looked vaguely familiar, stood unnoticed and alone. Who was he? I tried to place him. With a leap of heart I recognized him from newspaper pictures—it was Willkie. I went over and introduced myself to him. His grin spread in warmth all over his rugged face, and he took my hand in his two great paws as he expressed his admiration and fondness for my husband.

I told him I had listened to him on the radio when he appeared on "Information Please." His appearance on that program had been so successful that the public had begun to talk of him as presidential timber for the Republicans. No one in Washington took this talk seriously. Willkie had been a registered Democrat, not a Republican, until a few months before. He had no organization, no political qualifications. He had been born in Indiana. He had fought the battle against Roosevelt and the Tennessee Valley Authority for the power utilities. That was about all that was known about him. Not by the farthest stretch of practical political imagination could you figure a way by which he could get the presidential nomination!

I liked him at once. Gaily, I told him I had been on a local "Information Please" program recently. I bet him he could not correctly answer the question which I had failed. "What state in the United States extends farthest north?" Like a flash he answered correctly, "Minnesota."

I then told him of my pet project of that moment—a series of lectures on foreign affairs, which some of us were conducting. Would he come to speak for us? He would be glad to come, he promised.

At this point, someone else came up to speak to me and Willkie escaped to another room where my husband next discovered him alone in a corner. Willkie said, "I'm hiding from your wife. I answered correctly a quiz question she asked me, and I'm afraid she'll think up another I can't answer."

A few nights later, we saw him again at an editor's banquet, when he debated the third-term issue with Harold Ickes. We sat just below the speakers' table. Willkie spotted me at once and leaned over to greet us, shouting, "Minnesota!" After that, he always greeted me with that expression.

Two years later, after he had made his wartime trip to Russia and China, I went up to New York to plead with him again to come to speak in Constitution Hall to the great audience of "The United Nations Lecture Series," of which I was chairman. It was three days after Christmas. I hated to leave my children—home from school for the holidays—to go to New York. But our committee keenly felt that the Republican standard bearer, just back from the war fronts, should be heard by this audience of diplomats, Congressional leaders, and government people.

When I walked into his Wall Street office, he greeted me most cordially. "Minnesota, you haven't come all the way to New York at Christmas time just to ask me to make a speech, have you?" Well, he was not going to make any speeches. He was writing a book; he was very busy—writing was difficult for him; and, besides, he hated Washington. Every time he came down people gathered about and whispered terrible things in his ears about "that man, Roosevelt" which nauseated him. Here we were fighting a desperate war for survival, and all Roosevelt's opposition did was to peddle gossip about the Commander-in-Chief.

He talked on about his fatigue and mentioned other excuses until I became furious with him. Suddenly I lashed out at him as I had never talked to anyone except my husband, when I wanted to goad him on to greater effort. In substance I said:

"You tell me you are too tired. Your son, Philip, spent Christmas day on a ship in dangerous waters. He is tired, too. We are all tired. Philip's tiredness does not prevent him from doing his duty. You have a far greater duty—the duty to take the leadership in establishing a new world order, so that never again need boys like Philip spend Christmas in dangerous, submarine-infested waters. At the moment, Roosevelt does not seem to be taking this leadership. No one is. I don't know whether you'll ever sit in the White

House or not. I don't care. But destiny at this moment offers you a golden opportunity to say what is deep in your heart to an audience of the world, such as you'd find no place else in the world. But 'No!' you say. . . . You are too tired!"

I was so furious I rose to my feet to leave.

"Wait," he laughed, "let me try to rearrange my schedule." He leaned back in his chair and howled with laughter at me. "I'll try—really I will—and I'll send you a wire tomorrow, telling you whether or not I can come."

I returned to Washington and received next day a telegram:

"DEAR OLIVE: TRULY I CAN'T MAKE IT. THE BOOK COMES FIRST. THANKS FOR THE TALKING-TO YOU GAVE ME. REGARDS TO RAY. WENDELL."

Of course I forgave him when I read his *One World*.

The constructive service which Wendell Willkie performed for the country in 1940 was that he took his stand with President Roosevelt on foreign policy, and in so doing crossed many of his own party leaders, who wanted to use foreign policy as a partisan football.

Mr. Willkie also brought into sharp focus the basic arguments between the New Dealers and private capitalism. He believed that private capitalism could carry the ball alone. The New Dealers believed that was inadequate, and that public spending must supplement it. Mr. Willkie promised that industry if given its head could provide jobs for all. He had a deep, unshakable conviction that accounted for the personal vitality which stirred him to fight doggedly in his crusade.

Tomatoes and eggs along with insults were flung in Willkie's face time and again, but he campaigned with the undaunted fervor of an evangelist. Right or wrong, rugged conviction lay behind his earnestness. He almost burst his larynx in his attempt to make all the nation listen to his passionate conviction that private capitalism was adequate to the job of creating a modern world of machine power.

After all was said and done, there was only one real issue in the 1940 campaign—to obtain the fastest possible industrial production for our defense. We faced a serious international situation. We were practically defenseless and exposed in a world at war.

Like many others, my husband felt that President Roosevelt had a heritage of such bitterness with our industrial leaders that he would never be able to secure their cooperation in this production program. He felt that Wendell Willkie could more expertly merge all opposing groups in a close-knit unity.

One week before the election, my husband went up to New York to write and broadcast about the Empire State's pivotal situation in the election. The night he left Washington, his column appeared announcing that he personally favored the election of Wendell Willkie. It was a shock to me, though I knew the hours of soul-searching he had gone through to come to this conclusion. He had believed ardently in the domestic goals and achievements of President Roosevelt. He had often criticized his methods. By a slow process of struggle within himself, he finally reached the conclusion that the hours ahead for democracy would be tragic. If we were to survive at all, the first requisite was national unity. Willkie, he believed, could bring this about.

I was actively working in the Democratic Party in Maryland. My husband had never before supported any candidate or any political party. I was both angry and hurt when he threw the weight of his influence to Willkie.

I drove him to the Union Station, the night he left for New York. We didn't argue the issues any longer. Our hearts were heavy, and the world seemed to hang on the thin edge of a precipice.

When I returned home after putting him on the train, I found a telegram at the house, addressed to him from Clare Booth Luce, speaker for and strong supporter of Willkie. As I remember it, it read:

"NO MATTER WHAT HAPPENS NEXT TUESDAY (ELECTION DAY) YOU AND I WILL KNOW THAT WE WERE RIGHT. I INTEND TO QUOTE YOUR COLUMN TONIGHT ON THE RADIO. HOPE YOU WILL LISTEN IN. YOU ARE JUST, JUST WONDERFUL."

I did not know Mrs. Luce personally at this time. I had heard of her great beauty and had marveled at her clever playwriting. I couldn't help feeling a little jealous of this glamorous woman who so effusively complimented my husband. Ray knew both Harry and Clare Luce quite well by this time, and although they had invited us to visit them for a week-end, I had not had the pleasure of meeting either of them.

In my jealousy of Mrs. Luce, and my disappointment over my husband's political stand, I sent him a night letter, quoting Mrs. Luce's telegram, tacking on at the end my own personal "No love, Olive." It amused my husband and restored my own equilibrium.

In later years, Clare Booth Luce became one of my most treasured friends. Naturally we never agreed politically, but I always felt the keenest appreciation for her political success as a woman.

Chapter Fourteen

TAKE ANOTHER LOOK
AT THE QUARTERBACK

WITH THE GROWING RUMORS THAT President Roosevelt would attempt to break the two-term tradition in the Presidency to seek a third term, it was necessary to take a second and deeper look at this man who had made friends and enemies with a prodigal hand. While the March of Dimes and the balls and parties were being given for the Infantile Paralysis Campaign which marked his fifty-eighth birthday, he was perceptibly grayer, but the cigarette in its holder was at the same jaunty angle after seven long years. He showed no evidence as he lounged at his knick-knack-covered desk that the Presidency had him licked. He laughed and exchanged repartee with the best wisecrackers; his health was excellent, his spirits high; and he had enough stamina, it seemed, for another decade in active politics.

You had to see him close up to remember at all that he had been an invalid who had struggled seven long years to regain his health and who was unable to walk alone. To the world, he was the symbol of democracy and his life was the material of which historic epics were written. Year in and year out, his colored valet brought his breakfast to him in bed at 8:30 A.M., and, like most men, he was not very cheerful until after he had eaten and smoked a cigarette. He shaved himself. He read five morning newspapers. He swam with a powerful stroke in the White House pool almost daily, on the way home from the office wing.

He was an informal dresser, clinging tenaciously to old suits for comfort. He had an altercation with the Gridiron Club over their requirement that all their guests wear white ties to the semi-annual dinners. He wanted to substitute the less formal black ties. He said it was the first time he had known that people depended on a high hat, white tie, and tails for entertainment. George Holmes, the 1938 president of the Gridiron Club, answered that as far as people were concerned they didn't get much help out of a black tie, either. The sentiment of the club was for keeping the tradition intact, and they felt that he had an obsession on the question. It could have been that Roosevelt found a soft shirt easier when he was negotiating the long walk up to the head table. Roosevelt always arrived at his place at the dinner sweating and panting. He complained bitterly about having to speak at the dinners, instead of relaxing for a good time.

Millions of letters continually poured into the White House, but I am told that his favorite was one from a western farm wife who wrote:

"Dear Frank: Our neighbor loaned us twenty-five dollars on our team. He says he will take the mules unless he can come to see me when my husband is away. How can I save the mules?"

Once there was a rumor, which Paul Mallon printed in his column, that Henry Morgenthau, Secretary of the Treasury, was going to be sent as Ambassador to France. Roosevelt saw the story and wrote the following note to Morgenthau:

"Henry, see by the newspapers you are going to Paris. . . . As Al Smith is reported to have wired the Pope after the 1928 election—'Unpack!'"

Roosevelt loved to make puns. When he returned from his vacation in the spring of 1934, after the House of Representatives had been conducting the Wirt Investigation of the charges that Rexford Tugwell, assistant Secretary of Agriculture, was a Communist and that the brain trusters were plotting a revolution in the country, Roosevelt said to the delegation of Congressmen who greeted him at the station upon arrival, "I hear you have been going from bad to Wirt."

Roosevelt never locked his door at night. He had a certain fatalism and believed that if he was to die from an assassin's bullet, no precautions that could be taken would prevent it. There was one gate-crashing incident that we knew about at the White House, which Mrs. Morgenthau related to me.

They had been asked to the family New Year's Eve party at the White House, and Mrs. Roosevelt had told the Morgenthaus to have their children drop in later in the evening to wish their parents a "Happy New Year." This they had arranged to do. When Mrs. Morgenthau arrived at the White House, she explained to the usher at the door that her daughter and a young man or two would arrive late in the evening, probably in a Ford, and asked that they be sent upstairs.

Toward midnight a Ford did drive up, and a boy and a girl jumped out. They walked through the door, with the usher naturally supposing it was the Morgenthau youngsters. A motion picture was being shown upstairs in the family living room. The boy and girl stood in the doorway until the light came on. Then the young man walked over to the President and asked for his autograph, saying that his school had asked him to get it to help raise money for the Warm Springs Foundation.

Roosevelt looked amazed. Mrs. Roosevelt looked puzzled, but said later that she thought that Mrs. Morgenthau had arranged it. Mrs. Morgenthau looked puzzled, thinking Mrs. Roosevelt had arranged it. The President said he would have to go out to his study and get a pen and sit at his desk to sign. His aide took him out, and the boy accompanied them. As they left the room, Secretary Morgenthau asked who the youngster was. Nobody seemed to know, so he rushed out to the study, where he found Roosevelt alone with the young man. Morgenthau burst into the room, went up to the boy, who was leaning close over Roosevelt, and said, "How did you get in here?" The boy said that he had just walked in. Morgenthau said, "You have no right to do this," and hustled the boy and girl downstairs and out. They climbed into the Ford and drove off, yelling back at the Secret Service, "Guess that's putting one over on you!"

After that, the White House exercised the strictest precautions, allowing no one upstairs unless vouched for. Invitation cards which formally included a ticket of admission to the White House were sent out, and the admission card was withheld until the invitation had been accepted.

Once in a while a newspaper correspondent would get the better of Roosevelt, as happened in 1938 at a budget conference with the press. While the President waited for the crowd of newspapermen to get settled, Roosevelt looked at Walter Trohan, the Chicago *Tribune* White House correspondent, and in kidding contempt said, "Huh! Financial writer!" Trohan laughed, picked up the budget, opened it and said to the President, "Huh! Balanced budget, eh?" Roosevelt didn't seem to like it.

I was always interested in the relationship between the President and his energetic wife, who not only brought him through his infantile paralysis but also, with the help of Louis Howe and James Farley, made him President of the United States. Mrs. Roosevelt was the President's eyes, ears, and legs. She saw more people every year in her travels than six Presidents could see. She always reported all her findings to him.

Far from being a beautiful woman, Eleanor Roosevelt nevertheless impressed everyone who met her with such sincerity and charm that her visitors would remark, "Why, she is a lovely person." She possessed an unpleasant high-keyed voice which she has trained to pleasantness. If she became excited it broke out of bounds and the old shrill arpeggios would scream forth.

The dynamo that drove her was a powerful conviction that every man and woman must have opportunity to develop to their highest potential. Crusaders usually think in terms of a law to be passed or a goal to be reached. Mrs. Roosevelt was not so much a crusader for causes as she was an indignant champion of the downtrodden individual. She wanted everybody to have a decent home, an education, a fair chance. She cannot endure the presumption that some individuals or groups of individuals are inferior to others. It is not a love of dark-skinned or yellow-skinned or any color-of-skin people that motivates her fight for racial tolerance. It is just that she cannot endure unfairness, unequal opportunities, discrimination. She sees human beings who need to be mothered and helped. This is the reason the attacks on her do not disturb her. They don't even reach or touch her personally. Venomous language leveled at her finds her impervious. She simply doesn't think of herself, importantly or otherwise.

Wendell Willkie wrote to me when he was under blistering attacks in the press that he wished he could take those attacks on himself as imperturbably as Eleanor Roosevelt did and wondered what her secret of endurance was. I think it stems from exceptional humility plus her belief that she could improve herself and her program from this criticism.

Most women mother a child or two. Mrs. Roosevelt mothered the world. She lived and spoke for the "forgotten" women. In the far reaches of these United States, in the slums of great cities, on the forsaken farms, and in the factories are millions of forgotten women. They found a friend in Eleanor Roosevelt. They could read in the daily papers what she did and what she believed. They could even write to her in their extreme need. She would read their letters. What is more, she would try to do something for them. She might even try to turn the cumbersome wheels of legislation or bureaucracy a little faster in order to bring them justice, calling down upon her own head the angry outbursts of those who have forgotten the weak and lonely, those who do not remember the quality of mercy.

The job in the White House grew in her twelve years there to include a woman-sized job as well as a man-sized job.

Like other married couples, Franklin and Eleanor Roosevelt had their disagreements. There was a persistent rumor of a love affair in the early twenties. Mrs. Roosevelt was reported to have called her husband and the enamored woman to a conference, at which she offered to give her husband a divorce if the woman wished to marry him. A Catholic, the woman could not marry a divorced man. When she expressed these sentiments, Mrs. Roosevelt issued an ultimatum that they must stop seeing each other—to which they promptly acquiesced. For a man as handsome and gay as

Franklin Roosevelt, it is interesting that he was singularly free from entanglements with the feminine sex.

I remember in 1935 Dr. Cary Grayson's saying that Mrs. Roosevelt was the real boss at the White House. In substantiation, he said that Roosevelt asked him if he knew how to get rid of a dog. Grayson said he did, and Roosevelt explained that one of the White House dogs had bitten three people, including Senator Hattie Caraway, but the dog belonged to Mrs. Roosevelt and she refused to let him go. The President said, however, that if he bit another person he was going to get rid of him. The dog promptly bit two other people, but it still remained at the White House.

Mr. and Mrs. Roosevelt did not always agree on social legislation. Some advocates of old-age pensions were urging Mrs. Roosevelt in 1932 to persuade her husband to come out in favor of pensions. She told them that some one else would have to talk to Franklin about it, because the two of them had argued the subject so extensively that they were not on speaking terms about it.

Consumed with interest in the debate over Roosevelt and a third term we talked often and long about it with the Donald Richbergs. They had just returned from England, where Don had visited former Premier Lloyd George in Surrey, forty miles from London, at his large rambling home. Lloyd George was in his middle seventies, but he came bustling out to meet Don, full of pep and energy. He launched into a discussion of the third-term-for-Roosevelt possibility and said:

Take Another Look at the Quarterback

"I can't understand Americans being opposed to it. Here you have as head of your government the only man in the world who speaks to the whole world with the authentic voice of democracy. He is a very great man. . . . Why do you want to throw him out? Why give up the services of a man so valuable? I listen to and read every word he utters, because it is the authentic voice of democracy speaking. Please explain this phenomenon to me."

Don replied in substance that he couldn't give a very rational explanation, except that the feeling was very deep-rooted. As a matter of fact, there was very little justification, historically, against a President's running a third time. The Constitution contains nothing on the subject. George Washington set the precedent because he was tired; he thought he had done enough and wanted to retire to Mount Vernon.

Don explained that a great many people feared the perpetuation of a President in office as a sign of dictatorship; furthermore, they feared a powerful patronage machine. Lloyd George snorted at this and said patronage amounted to nothing. Don said, "Our Presidency is the most powerful office among the democracies." Lloyd George disagreed, pointing out that the Prime Minister has much more power, that there is absolutely no curb at all as long as he holds his majority in Parliament, whereas we have the Supreme Court to invalidate laws, the Senate to confirm appointments, and a lot of other constitutional checks.

They talked about many other subjects, but as Don was leaving Lloyd George grabbed him by the arm and said,

"You give your President a message for me. . . . You tell him I think he ought to run for a third term. Tell him to run."

When Donald Richberg gave Roosevelt the message from Lloyd George, Roosevelt went into a long recital of the history of one-man political movements. Lasting movements, he said, were not one-man affairs. They were party and organization efforts. He pointed out how Theodore Roosevelt failed in 1912 and La Follette in 1924. Such one-man movements vanish when the leader is removed. F.D.R. was not interested in founding a Roosevelt Party but wanted to make the Democratic Party as liberal as possible and hold it together.

Every man who has ever worked with Roosevelt agrees that he was a fast worker when at his desk. In the NRA days, Don would go in to see the President, who would have a huge stack of mail and papers to sign before him. "Missy" Le Hand would be standing by. One by one, at a rapid pace, he would glance over the papers and say, "Do this, do that. . . . Tell him this. Tell him that—" as fast as he could go. While this was going on, Don would continue talking to the President and sometimes wondered how much Roosevelt had heard of what he was saying. Sometimes Roosevelt would stop in the middle of it, push all the papers away from him, lean back in his chair, relax completely, and say, "Don, did I ever tell you the story of so-and-so?" He'd talk for ten minutes, completely free from official care. Richberg always thought that only by such ability to toss off his problems could a man stand the Presidency.

Once when Don was worried about something, Roosevelt, cautioning against worry, recalled a remark Woodrow Wilson once made during World War I. Roosevelt, Assistant Secretary of the Navy, was terribly worried over something, and Wilson said, "I think we will both find that many of the things we worry most about and work hardest over will be forgotten in history; but some little detail, which we are completely passing over as a trifle, will be seized upon and become our monument." Perhaps he was thinking of Lincoln's Gettysburg Address.

The chief trouble with Roosevelt was that he tended to dwarf all other men around him. He was such a strong man that nobody else seemed to have the necessary stature when placed beside him. If, by any chance, a man gave evidence of growing up to presidential stature, Roosevelt inevitably got rid of him.

Roosevelt himself never changed. He couldn't. He was a Roosevelt, and the Roosevelt blood is strong, driving with abounding, restless energy.

Once some one told him a story about Coolidge. When Coolidge was Governor of Massachusetts, he saw a great many visitors yet was always able to leave his office early. His successor found that callers were taking all of his time; even so, he was unable to see as many visitors as had Coolidge. This worried him, so he asked Coolidge how he had managed them. Coolidge answered, "When they came in to see me, I didn't talk back." Roosevelt enjoyed the story, but he didn't take the hint. He could no more be quiet and study his lesson than a healthy small boy could resist wiggling, jumping up, banging here, banging there. He loved a fight, he had to have action.

He had had plenty of it since the day in 1933 when he first stood on the east steps of the Capitol and took over guidance of a nation that had suffered a complete breakdown. During those years, my husband had seen the New Deal unfold in its early glory of great promise. He had reported the long struggle with powerful, hostile forces, seen and unseen —economic and human. He had seen the sudden recession of 1937; he'd seen the New Deal morale disintegrate. Through all of this time he had seen Roosevelt—sometimes up, sometimes down—striking now with all the daring of genius, and, again, blundering into appalling errors, which needlessly undermined the great work he was trying to do, playing cruelly into the hands of his enemies. Roosevelt was the fifth President whose activities my husband reported. None had been perfect, certainly not Roosevelt. Yet, to Ray Clapper, Roosevelt stood as a giant of our time, for the mark of a great man is not an absence of weakness but an abundance of strength. He liked best to describe him as "a living example of democracy, who tried to subdue the ugly facts of society to some more rational scheme of things, who wanted to bring about in his time a world which would venture some few paces on into the vistas of hope, which science and man's ingenuity had opened up to us. . . ."

Take Another Look at the Quarterback

Roosevelt's championship of the "forgotten man" was a social worker's point of view: mend, put on a patch here and there, get a job for every one, see that they are not hungry, build houses, improve health, et cetera. It had absolutely nothing to do with ideologies. He thought the democratic capitalistic system could be made to work. If you spell out every bit of legislation, every executive order, you will find they add up to an attempt to modernize the house, not to destroy it.

Even when Roosevelt was ill, suffering from his periodic sinus attacks, he was a gay and amusing host. I remember one small dinner party at the White House in May, 1939, when the President kept us in gales of laughter by telling story after story. He told about a trip he took to Paris when he was Assistant Secretary of the Navy during the First World War. The French newspapermen requested a press conference at ten o'clock one morning. They arrived dressed up in morning coats and black ties, as though for a diplomatic reception. Roosevelt, in informal clothes, sat on the edge of a desk talking to them. One French newspaperman asked him if it was true that members of the Cabinet in the United States received the press every day.

"Oh, yes," answered Roosevelt. "Sometimes during wartime they see the newspapermen twice a day."

"Mon Dieu," they said.

Roosevelt thought little of it, but the next morning he had a breakfast engagement with Premier Clemenceau in a little room in the Foreign Office. Clemenceau had been at work since 6 A.M. Roosevelt entered; Clemenceau rose and came toward him in a menacing, snarling manner that scared Roosevelt. He crouched and made claw-like movements with his fingers, saying in evident seriousness:

"What have you done to me? You force me to resign today. If I resign, we lose the war. . . . It is your fault we lose the war."

In astonishment Roosevelt asked what had happened.

Clemenceau said: "Your interview with the French newspapermen yesterday . . . they tell me you hold daily press conferences and they demand the same from me! I refuse! I have not time to see the press daily. I resign! My government falls. We lose the war!"

At that same dinner, Roosevelt also said many amusing things in connection with arrangements which were being made for the impending visit of the King and Queen of Great Britain. It seemed every problem about their visit was being dumped into his lap, but he was especially proud of solving one question Solomon-wise.

For forty years, since the United States first had had ambassadors, protocol had ruled that there never could be an ambassador and a chief justice of the United States at the same dinner. Ambassadors rank in protocol only beneath the President and the Vice President of the United States; but at the state dinner which the President and Mrs. Roosevelt were giving in honor of the King, both the British Ambassador and the Chief Justice of the United States had to be seated. The problem was so grave that the State Department couldn't solve it and passed the buck to Roosevelt. As the President told us gaily:

"I worked out the real solution, and they are kicking themselves over at the State Department that they didn't think of it. Ambassador Lindsey bore the title, 'Envoy Extraordinary and Minister Plenipotentiary.' This was a dual role. He represented the King in person as Envoy Extraordinary; but, as Minister, he represented the government. Since the King would be present at the dinner in person, there was no reason why Lindsey should be present as Ambassador. He was to come only as the Minister representing his government. As such, he could be seated below the Chief Justice."

From these and other gay stories Roosevelt told that night, I doubt that any of us realized that the President was in pain. I sat beside Steve Early, press secretary, who told me that Roosevelt was at that moment running a temperature and that the doctor thought he ought to stay in bed. When we left the dining room, the President in his wheel chair got into the elevator and went directly to his bedroom. A few minutes later, the doctor told Mrs. Roosevelt that he had ordered the President to bed because his temperature was rising.

During the early part of 1939 President Roosevelt gave the reporters at the press conference a severe scolding. For a half-hour he railed at them about purposeful misrepresentations, calling them "purveyors of pure bunk . . .

B-U-N-K." The cause of the dressing-down of the press was not any misdemeanor which the newspapermen themselves had committed. He charged the press with deliberate lying in news stories about his attitude on international relations. This was the first wide-open break between newspapermen and the President. The history of the incident went back to a star-chamber session, which Roosevelt held with a group of Republican and Democratic Congressional leaders. According to the Congressmen, Roosevelt pledged them not to reveal what he said to them about the grave international situation. Roosevelt characterized this pledge of secrecy as 100 percent b-u-n-k. No matter who was to blame, the story of the session leaked. From what newspapermen were able to learn, Roosevelt had said in substance at the session:

"We are dealing with a mad man (in Germany), and we have to treat him as such. Ordinary methods of dealing with rational men don't work in this case. The situation will never be righted until Hitler is assassinated." The Congressional leaders agreed that Roosevelt used the word "righted" but they were not sure that he urged assassination. This was the session at which Roosevelt named the Rhine River as the defensive frontier between totalitarian states and democracy.

Westbrook Pegler summed up the President's conduct with the press in this instance as follows: "Our President stepped on a rake and the handle hopped up and hit him in the eye. He then blamed the press for leaving the rake lying around but, hell, Paw . . . you done left that rake there your own se'f."

Chapter Fifteen

A WAR THAT WAS
NONE OF OUR BUSINESS

T HE YEAR 1940 UNFOLDED IN SHROUDS of pessimism. But a faith reached out and took hold of us—a belief in America. We had not found satisfactory solutions to our problems but one great truth emerged. We knew without a doubt that our democracy offered individual freedom and opportunity—a way of life incomparably beyond anything that other systems of government had offered. Hitler had shown us the evils of dictatorship; Russia, the afflictions of communism. And between these, democracy shone with a new brilliance. Life was free and secure. We were deeply blessed by Providence.

But our way of life allowed full freedom for all the orneriness in human nature. We had pettiness in officials, crookedness in local governments, a reluctance on the part of everyone to jump into our defense requirements. Enlistments in the Army lagged, business refused to expand for greater production, and labor racketeers fattened on the confusion of bureaucracy.

Never had life dangled so much opportunity within reach

of the average man. A comfortable life was in sight for everyone and the means of attaining it was dependent on the satisfactory functioning of private capitalism.

But private capitalism was still sick. The stagnation which plagued the country for a decade had its origin back in the Hoover days, when individual enterprise ruled the roost and there were no New Dealers prowling around. We were edging into state socialism while trying to salvage private capitalism. The survival of democracy was largely a question of whether or not we could arrange a middle ground with sufficient speed and skill while the world was rapidly going totalitarian. It wasn't a question of good intentions but a test of competency we faced.

A world going totalitarian. Few of us comprehended the meaning of that phrase. For months the war in Europe seemed phony, stalemated, locked in inaction.

I remember lunching at the Willard Hotel in Washington one day with Virgil Pinckley, manager of the United Press in Europe. He was frantic with consternation. He had been on a lecture trip across the United States and had learned how little we comprehended Germany's intentions and the threat to our way of life. How to arouse the United States? That was the urgent question on the lips of our correspondents, newspapermen, and diplomats. If you "Paul Revered" them, you were accused of war-mongering. You were abused, taunted and threatened. Quentin Reynolds, William Shirer, Vincent Sheean, John Gunther, Ed Beattie —all our top-flight men in Europe knew our peril.

A War That Was None of Our Business

Looking back today, from the pinnacle of our victory, on that struggle of public opinion within the United States, it is hard to believe that there was so much bitterness. Raymond Clapper's stand was in reality a very mild one: he believed in help to Britain and France short of actually sending an army. Yet his life was threatened, as were our children's lives; we were subjected to indignities, hundreds of filthy, profane letters.

One night during the fight to revise the Neutrality Pact, I was invited to participate in a radio debate on the subject. The broadcast originated in a downstairs room at the Mayflower Hotel, so that the public could be present. Mrs. Gifford Pinchot and I debated in favor of repeal; Dorothy Detzer of the Women's International League for Peace and Freedom and Florence Boeckel of the National Council for the Prevention of War opposed us. We were all old friends, and the debate was intelligent and tolerant.

Toward the end, a large group of frowsy, belligerent women entered. The moment we went off the air, one group of eight or ten of them surrounded me, another group cornered Mrs. Pinchot. These were the women who called themselves "Mothers of America," or some such misnomer. They had been picketing Congress; had hung Senator Claude Pepper of Florida in effigy; and one of them had appeared in the House Gallery wearing a skull mask. They had resorted to all kinds of grotesque methods to get publicity to keep the United States from helping the democracies.

A War That Was None of Our Business

The group attacking me closed in in a menacing manner, all shouting belligerent questions at me simultaneously. The tumult they made was out of all proportion to their number. I was on the platform, a step or two above them. I listened a few minutes, until they began shaking their fists in my face. "Why don't you answer us?" they screamed.

I hate fights, and I am an awful coward. I murmured, "If you'll be quiet a minute I'll try." They had to stop yelling to hear my soft words. Then I said, "Look, I'll be glad to talk with any one of you or any two, if you'll come to see me quietly, where we can talk. I refuse to be badgered this way." With a lunge downward, I stepped through their midst, walked to the rear of the room and out. They recovered their breath and followed. One ran in front of me and spat in my face. I took out my handkerchief, wiped my face, and took the arm of a Jewish Congressman, who asked, "Mrs. Clapper, can my wife and I escort you to your car?" Up the stairs and out through the lobby we calmly walked as they followed us, yelling at me, "Jew-lover!"

I knew that a hair-pulling fight for publicity purposes was exactly what they craved. That would have been grist for their mill. These poor women must have been hirelings of someone. They could not have paid their own railroad fare to Washington. All of them were obviously very poor and ignorant, and they spoke in broken English. Their tactics were to intimidate and abuse.

After being hanged in effigy by these same women, Senator Pepper's speech of acceptance was a beautiful gem, a classic utterance, breathing the spirit of our free democracy. He said: "Knowing these women, like all other Americans, are sincere in their patriotism, placing America first and Hitler last, I feel that their hanging me in effigy is a splendid demonstration of what we are all trying to preserve—freedom of speech and freedom of action in the American way of doing things. I only hope that the spectators and those who hear about this business will feel that I also love America, and that I am sincere in my daily efforts to defend the United States in liberty, the right of free speech and free action."

Bravo, Claude Pepper. Abe Lincoln could not have said it better.

The phony war lasted until the spring thaws came in 1940. In a twinkling second, Norway fell in Hitler's blitz, then Denmark, Belgium, Holland. But France—oh, yes, France would hold as she had in the gallant rally of spirit in World War I, when the taxicabs of Paris carried her fighting reserves to halt the German advance. Yearning, breathless, we listened to the hourly radio reports of the retreat of the French and British armies. Confusion, headlong flights of frantic civilians, unearthly strafing from the skies—back, back fell the Allied armies before the enemy.

France fallen. Dunkerque! The mind staggered and reeled as the French signed armistice terms.

Then it was Britain alone.

A War That Was None of Our Business

Britain, with the lion heart of Winston Churchill—blood, sweat, and tears.

With our hearts in our mouths, we the sleepwalkers awoke. The timid spectators of a war "that was none of our business" looked to Uncle Sam's defenses. They were not much to look at. And it was suddenly later than we had thought.

Our regular Army, when France fell, had been increased to 280,000 men, slightly over a quarter of a million men. That number of men made eight triangular divisions and our first armored division. The Air Force was being brought up to a 25 group program of 105 tactical squadrons. We were beginning to train 7,000 pilots a year. As Secretary Stimson said, we had an Army only in the sense that one was in the process of production. The same was true of our Air Force. We were pitifully low on small-arms ammunition and powder. We did possess a powerful Navy, which with the British Navy operating in our interest was greatly in our favor. At the rate German submarines were sinking British craft, however, this advantage was threatened. Of all shortages, probably the worst were in materials like rubber and tin.

At the end of the year 1940, defense production was in a terrible slump. William S. Knudsen, head of the Defense Commission, made no effort to conceal the lag in production. Straight out, he told us that out of the hoped for production of a thousand airplanes per month, we were actually producing only 30 percent.

Brigadier General George V. Strong said in 1940 that we

ere strong in the Western Hemisphere as long as two conditions were maintained. First, the Panama Canal must be
safe from attack by surface vessels or land forces. There was
always the off chance of a suicide dash to drop a load of
bombs on some part of it, but the real danger was from
sabotage. Second, no aggressor must be allowed a base from
which to operate in the Western Hemisphere—from New-
foundland to Rio de Janeiro in the east, from Alaska to
Australia in the west.

The sad state of defense in Alaska illustrated how Congress had neglected defense. There were two companies of
infantry at Haines, Alaska, the tip of the Inside Passage, a
post established forty years before, during the Klondike
Gold Rush. In 1937 the Navy started work on air bases at
Sitka and Kodiak Islands. In all Alaska, there was not a
single airfield capable of safely handling the take-off of our
largest bombers. The War Department had asked for twelve
million dollars to establish an air base at Anchorage, but was
turned down by Congress. This action was reversed when
Hitler took the Low Countries. Alaska, with its small population, could have been invaded easily by parachute troops.
It could have been held by a comparatively small force,
which would have been difficult to dislodge.

We found it hard to comprehend the size of our job. We
simply could not understand the enormous scope of total
war. We hesitated, squirmed, and reached for soft decisions.

This was not owing to any lack of patriotism or willingness to do the job, but to our basic "shut in" character. We

also suffered from auto-intoxication and a split personality, part of us still clinging to the idea that we wouldn't get into any trouble unless we went looking for it.

The mind of the American people found the slow-motion menace of Fascism screened from a clear view. It has always been the American way to be rather slow in discovering what our task is. During the Civil War, Union preparations were almost fatally slow. Again in the First World War, we were slow in starting. Our danger never was that we could not do a job. It was that we were slow in waking up to what had to be done.

As a nation, we always do a job when we believe that it really must be done. We did not believe we were actually in any danger. In this respect, we were not much different from the British and the French who wanted peace so desperately that they failed to prepare. Just as we believed that we were safe behind the Atlantic Ocean, so the French believed they were safe behind their Maginot Line. Had the American people really understood dictatorships and totalitarian war, they probably would have made an early entry into the conflict. By so doing, World War II would have been immeasurably shortened, because once our mighty production ability got going, it swung the balance of might.

While all this was going on to hasten our defense preparations, there was much talk spreading through the Middle West, stimulated by the Chicago *Tribune*, of the desirability of a deal with Japan. The idea was that to prevent the totalitarian powers from ganging up on us, we should placate

Japan and make an ally of her. Thus, if it became necessary to face Germany, we would have Japan a loyal friend at our back. To sell out to Japan at that time would have meant turning adrift Australia, New Zealand, the Philippines, and the Dutch East Indies. We would have had to put the seal of our approval upon such a betrayal and scuttle our traditional policy of friendship with China. Furthermore, it would have been a tip-off to all Latin America that the third great democracy was on the run.

We may have felt the importance of securing Latin America against Nazi domination, but some of our Latin neighbors, rightly or wrongly, feared increase of the power of the United States. I remember a small luncheon Oscar Chapman gave for the Mexican Secretary of State, Dr. Belata, which Ray attended, bringing home to me a very unhopeful picture. Dr. Belata was quite candid about the reaction of the Latin American Republics to our taking over bases in the Western Hemisphere. On the theory that Latin America would profit from a balance of power as between the United States and Germany, he said most of our neighbors would feel easier about German power than further American power. Most of our neighbors drew no parallel between their own possible fate and the fate of Norway and Holland. They wanted no North American encroachments and, except for Mexico, said Dr. Belata, practically every country was inclined to play ball with Germany.

The Germans operated airplanes in Ecuador, Colombia and Brazil. In two northern Latin American countries, German pilots and personnel operated within 250 miles of the Panama Canal. It was important that we be covered at least by friendly air bases and competent fleets within a thousand mile range of the Canal. Our first task was to sell Latin America the idea that it was for their protection as well as ours. But while State Department negotiations went on, Congress burst out in obstruction. With a sigh we recalled that the Germans didn't have to worry about any such embarrassing backfire at home.

Painfully, slowly, we saw that this was actually a world revolution to overthrow capitalist democracy everywhere. Germany intended to use Italy and Japan as her left and right hands to achieve world domination. When Mussolini declared war, he used these significant phrases: "Black Shirts of the Revolution . . . we take the field against the plutocratic and reactionary democracies. . . . This gigantic conflict is only a phase of the logical development of our Revolution. . . . It is a conflict between two ages, two ideas . . . an event of import for the centuries."

In such a situation as confronted us, we could trust only our own force. The thought that a deal with Japan would give us security was as false and treacherous as deceit itself. Our first job was to get busy immediately to become the strong neighbor in the Western Hemisphere, because no neighbor in this period was a good neighbor unless he was strong.

So we started out of the shadows, as Germany prepared the most devastating attack in all history upon England.

A War That Was None of Our Business

Earlier, Britain had been stunned and unable to cope with the aggressive tactics of Hitler but now the men and women of England were ready for it. Friends said their last good-byes to each other as they made ready to fight until death. Mercilessly, England's ports were shattered one by one, her war industries smashed daily. Darkness of heart and mind settled over the island that gave the Bill of Rights to mankind.

One of the most poignant phases of this period was the evacuation of England's children to her countrysides and to Canada and the United States. One night at dinner I talked with the British Ambassador, Lord Lothian, about increasing the number of children being brought over here to escape the bombings. Sadly he shook his head and told me that Britain could not spare convoy escorts and that the ships dare not cross the Atlantic without convoy. He seemed terribly worried and unhappy that night and gave the impression he saw no hope for his country's survival.

Lord Lothian, once a journalist himself, completely changed the character of the British Embassy in Washington, thawing it out for the first time in its long history. He gave informal luncheons and dinners, hired a good press relations man and insisted that attachés who ignored the press must change their attitude. When he came to Washington, relations between the Embassy and the press were bitter. When he died, they were better than the relations with any other diplomatic mission in town.

If Lord Lothian had been popular in Washington, his successor, Lord Halifax, became popular all over the United States. He was not so well-liked at first. He endured embarrassing insults when he went around the country to speak. In some instances, rotten eggs and tomatoes were thrown at him. But through the years of his diplomatic service here, he maintained such a tolerant, wise, and cheerful friendship with the people that his popularity greatly exceeds that of any other foreign diplomat.

Perhaps the most striking and unforgettable characteristic of Lord and Lady Halifax is their stoic acceptance of the tragedies which the war has brought into their personal lives. They have lost one son, and another son, David Wood, suffered amputation of both legs above the knee.

To my mind, the gallantry of this son, David Wood, learning to walk on steel legs, which require him to throw his large body from side to side in order to walk, is truly brave. One icy day not long ago, he was scheduled to visit the war-wounded at Forest Glen Hospital. The driveway leading to the hospital was so icy that his automobile could not make the grade. The wounded in the amputation wards gathered on their crutches in front of the window and witnessed the heroic effort of David Wood to climb that hill on his artificial legs. He stumbled repeatedly, but each time got up and made a new effort. Nothing he or anyone else could have said to these wounded men meant half as much as that agonizing climb he made up that hill to keep his appointment as he had promised.

Because the Halifaxes are a devoted and close-knit family,

there was no question about the depth of their grief about their sons, but they never stopped their ceaseless efforts to carry on in the best British tradition.

Lord Halifax took the trouble to travel all over this country, speaking in many places, presenting his government's tragic needs in the war years. He was wise enough never to say what he thought the United States should do. He never tried, by high diplomacy or low, to push American officials into any position. He assiduously molded a community of purpose between the British Commonwealth of Nations and the United States. He walked a tightrope well.

The British needed everything early in 1941. They particularly needed our Navy. Their port of Plymouth was badly damaged, and the town was so completely demolished that it had to be abandoned. Other port towns suffered the same heavy damage. They did not possess even one complete, fast-moving mechanized division. They desperately needed big tanks. All they had were light tanks, which could not be used against the heavy German tanks. The United States had barely begun production of the heavies, and it would be months before we could send any quantity.

The British had three months' supplies of food and were pleading for skimmed milk, dried eggs, dried fruit, juices, and concentrates. They were doing many ingenious things to save their water supply. Their health was good, but they knew that the real pinch would come the next winter, when the short rations would make a severe problem of food. The British people could take the bombings if their stomachs were full, but if they knew that there would be no food the next morning, they might have to quit. Germany, on the other hand, was able to live easier. Her people were disciplined in rationing. The "guns or butter" slogan had trained the nation in sacrifice.

Churchill needed our direct intervention. He could not understand why President Roosevelt could not move in with a free hand. He felt after Roosevelt's re-election that since Roosevelt was in the White House for four years and did not have to come before Congress every day as Churchill did before Parliament, that he should be willing to lead the country into direct intervention. It was pointed out to Churchill, however, that public opinion in the United States was so divided that Roosevelt feared the situation would turn against him. Without the support of public opinion, he would be as helpless and as repudiated as Wilson was in 1918. If Roosevelt lost his backing once, the jig was up for him. He could not move boldly.

On the other hand, Roosevelt faced the dilemma that if England did go down, there would be great panic in the United States. Roosevelt would be blamed for allowing it to happen. Churchill feared that if the British people ever got the idea that the United States was not coming in to help them, they would not stick. In fact, Lloyd George and some others were beginning to play the line that the United States was not coming in and that Great Britain had better quit. Churchill tried desperately to keep up the appearance that we were coming in by parading Ambassador Winant and other leading Americans as symbols.

I think we tend to forget the desperateness of the situation for the Western democracies a year after the fall of France. Marshal Petain was collaborating completely with Hitler, all the way. The Germans could have anything they wanted, including planes, men, and possibly the French fleet. As Under-Secretary of State Welles outlined to my husband, in May of 1941, although our basic interest was not to permit the Axis to get control in the Atlantic, we could not take any anticipatory action because that would appear as aggression. The immediate effect of any action on our part would be to force the Japanese to move into the war against us under their agreement with the Germans.

In an effort to clarify the final choice between intervention and non-intervention in this country, my husband drew up a number of questions which he asked his readers to consider. Cushman Reynolds, editor of *Uncensored*, reprinted the questions with answers that anti-interventionists might make. The list contained such questions as:

"Would you consider it a menace to the United States if Japan held Hawaii?"

"Would you feel that the United States had no cause for anxiety if the Axis took over the Azores, which are closer to our mainland than Hawaii?"

"If the Axis defeated England, would you favor occupying the Azores before the Axis established itself there?"

The answer given, which had a typically isolationist slant,

said that of course any move by the Axis endangered to some extent our national security, but that there was little reason to suppose that such dangers justified more economic or military intervention. The answer pointed out that whoever occupied strategic islands was open to easy attack and that from a military point of view it might be safer to let the Nazis or Japs occupy them. Then we could concentrate our own energy on being prepared to cut their supply lines, rather than to occupy these islands ourselves and run the danger of the Axis cutting our lines to these islands!

This soft, futile reply of the isolationists to this question showed their unrealistic knowledge of the tactics of modern war because later, during the war, the United States demonstrated that a powerful nation can use island bases for continental invasion very effectively.

Another question was, "If the Axis wins, do you think it would be easier or more difficult to carry on foreign trade?" "Do you think the Axis type of government-controlled barter trading would compel us to conduct our trade on a regimented basis, or do you think that foreign trade could still be conducted by private individuals, as at present?"

The isolationist answer to this was again one of skepticism. They said that foreign trade would be increasingly difficult to carry on anywhere; that foreign trade by private individuals, as at present and in the 19th Century, had a pretty gloomy future. They felt that everywhere, under fascism or democracy, the state was moving into business and commerce. Instead of showing a willingness to try to adjust for some measure of private industry and government control, they threw in the sponge, believed the world was hopelessly lost and nothing was worth any struggle whatsoever. They called this "realism."

This whole argument went on over and over again with bitter intensity, until finally the isolationist cause ran out of argument and crumbled to a point where there was only one weapon left—abuse. Lest we forget to what a low level democratic freedom of speech can descend, let me quote a few excerpts from letters of abuse sent to my husband. Don't expect them to make sense:

"You say that all rights and privileges of men have been added to rather than taken away. My answer to that is that you are a damned rabbit-footed, feather-legged, yellow-bellied liar. Is that clear? If that isn't clear, let me hear from you. . . . If you don't like it just meet me somewhere in the meadows of Virginia and I will wait on you just as Burr waited on Hamilton."

Another wrote, "I will not buy the paper again until its pages have been sterilized and fumigated from the smell of your putrid, low class, common, ungrammatical, uninteresting, untruthful, ignorant, half-witted, slimy outpourings. No loyalty to our dear country, no love for our flag, no adoration for our land do you show."

So the debate raged.

From the pinnacle of Allied victory in Europe in 1945, it is difficult to understand our own blindness to our danger.

A War That Was None of Our Business

I suppose the truth is that our minds, educated in democratic techniques, could not comprehend fascism. We tossed off as propaganda the stories of cruel concentration camps, we refused to believe Hitler's own statements of his philosophy of a super-race served by slave races. His threats to achieve world domination were looked upon as the ragings of an insane man.

Victor Hugo once said, "The greatest thing in the world is an idea whose time has come." Hitler's brain trusters knew that air power was the weapon that shrank the world to peanut size and the instrument that could control that peanut. His idea seemed to have come of age.

Although we didn't know it, the time had come when one or two powerfully productive nations could control the world. The Germans, through their geo-political theories and air power, got the jump on the rest of us. They came so close to accomplishing their domination that the mind still shivers at the narrow escape we had.

We didn't know at all what the war was all about. We were very dumb and slow. From our vantage point today, of course, we know what the real question was. Now we can spell out the very simple terms. Were Germany and her allies, with a totalitarian ideal, to control all mankind, or were the United States, Great Britain, and their friends to establish a cooperative world order?

The strength and potential power of the United States made inevitable our involvement. We were locked in a world room from which no one could escape. The desperadoes knew what was what. We did not. For a long time they slugged us right and left.

Who was to blame for our ignorance? It is easy to say that our leaders should have told us. Perhaps they did not put the case strongly enough. I'm inclined to think, however, that we, the people, have only ourselves to blame. We thought only of our own hides. The longer we waited, the deeper the blood bath became.

This issue of survival, this struggle between fascism and democracy, this fight-to-a-finish of slavery versus freedom was the primary focal issue brought on by the machine age. The Germans spelled it out for the world in huge black swastikas.

For the sake of a deeper understanding of ourselves in relationship to the new techniques of international relations brought on by a world that could be encircled from the air in five days, I would like to elaborate on the evolution of our policy in the thundering march of the Axis Powers toward world control.

On New Year's Day in 1941, no one could dare say what would happen in 1941. The tragic defeat which had been inflicted upon happy, prosperous, peaceful Scandinavia, the Low Countries, and France was only the prelude for the supreme decision between Germany and England. The United States had become an important but removed participant. Not through our wish, but because of our national interest, we slowly became the arsenal for Great Britain. If we want to be frank with ourselves, we must admit that we were lethargic in supplying the implements of war.

When my husband was in Great Britain in August and September, he found the results of our production program pitifully short of what was needed. We talked in big figures, but the bombers, tanks, and guns arrived in England in dribbling amounts. Only twenty flying fortresses, four of which were lost in crashes, and fifteen Airacobras had been delivered. For a long time we tried to keep up luxury production for civilian life. We didn't change our buying habits. We stalled on price control and rationing.

Yet our neutral days were over. Secretary Hull summed up the position of this government when he said, "We are not going to allow neutrality to chloroform us into inactivity regarding our defense." This was a milestone in the evolution of our policy toward the Axis.

As President Roosevelt took his oath of office on January 20, 1941, for his third term as President, the clouds which hung over that inaugural were as heavy as those that shadowed Lincoln's first. Though the American people faced a threat to their national security, they were as torn as they were in Lincoln's time, between a fervent wish that the threat would dissolve itself without our going to war and the fear that it would not. As then, the realities refused to shape themselves into any kind of compromise.

We saw the Axis states strong and menacing. Many thought democracy was doomed and, like Mrs. Anne Lindbergh in graceful and persuasive language, touched upon the physical comforts which modern tyrants sought to give their people. They obviously believed the German system rode the "wave of the future."

Not such a graceful picture was drawn by Hitler, when he said to Dr. Rauschning, "There will be a ruling class, tempered by battle and welded from the most varied elements. There will be the great hierarchy of the Party. And there will be the great mass of the anonymous, the serving collective, the eternally disenfranchised, no matter whether they were members of the old bourgeoisie, the big land owning class, the working class, or the artisans. Beneath them will still be the class of alien subject races; we need not hesitate to call them the modern slave class."

President Roosevelt in his inaugural speech challenged the idea that the wave of the future belonged to the totalitarian rulers. He believed democracy must ride that wave. All ancient struggles were a part of a current toward more freedom. "Democratic aspiration is human history," he said. He scorned the idea that man lives only for the state, always and totally.

Mr. Roosevelt breathed upon the "sacred fire of liberty," and turned it into a brighter glow. America had been in peril many times. It had been in peril from without and from within, but it had never retreated, not even when the odds were much against it. There has always been a spirit— greater, as Mr. Roosevelt said, than the sum of the parts— which had come through the shouting and doubting and kept the path of our faith lighted.

A War That Was None of Our Business

But, later, in May of 1941, when President Roosevelt proclaimed an unlimited national emergency, the first wave of reaction showed that he had failed to end the division inside the country. A group of non-interventionist Senators, including Burton K. Wheeler, Robert Taft, and Bennett Clark, met and resolved to continue their fight to keep the United States out of war. They drew up plans to carry on a campaign around the country and suggested an unofficial referendum or plebiscite of the nation.

This opposition exerted every effort to convince the American people that we did not need to do anything until the shooting actually reached American shores. For two years at least, we had had a long national debate on our war policy, but still the isolationists, from Charles Lindbergh down, used every pretext to divide the country.

When it seemed necessary to include Russia in the Lend-Lease program, these opponents tried to make a red herring out of Red Moscow. But Acting Secretary of State Welles struck hard and effectively at that kind of attempt to confuse the country. He voiced this country's dislike of the Communist dictatorship and of its suppression of religious and civil liberties, and made it clear that we had nothing in common except Hitler, the common enemy of both. Help from any source which would hasten the downfall of Hitler benefited our own security, he said.

These isolationists, these men who read with blind eyes and thought with limited imaginations, could visualize that at the end of a month Hitler might smash the Russian Army and be complete master of the rich storehouse of Western Russia. They could look on while Hitler, with such unlimited raw materials available to him, with millions of slave laborers, prepared to break out into the high seas. They knew he would not be content to remain landlocked.

Yet these men in positions of proud responsibility continued to advocate a negotiated peace with Hitler. They would have us sign a paper that would mean no more to Hitler than his other non-aggression pacts. It would only have lulled us to sleep while Germany prepared for new conquests.

In the meantime England held. Her winged warriors fought valiantly and died like flies. Hitler's bombers were not as effective as they thought, however. We could laugh at the joke going around of Adolf Hitler standing at Napoleon's tomb. He asked his aides to leave him, so that he could commune with the spirit of Napoleon. He stood looking at the tomb and suddenly it opened. Napoleon said, "Who are you?"

"I am Hitler, the conqueror," little Adolf answered.

"What have you conquered?" Napoleon asked.

"Austria, Czechoslovakia, Poland, Holland—even your own country France."

"Have you conquered England?"

"No," said Hitler.

"Then you might as well lie down here with me," sighed Napoleon.

In June, 1941, Hitler made his fatal play. He attacked Russia. He needed to nail down his food and oil supplies.

A War That Was None of Our Business

Perhaps Hitler felt unsafe and exposed for the climactic engagement with Britain, with Russia at his back. Soon he held the Russian Bear in a death grapple. His chances of busting Russia were very good. Her equipment was poor, her planes obsolescent, her officers poorly trained. What Russia had was hordes of strong, courageous fighting men with not much in their hands for a stand-up fight.

The logic that moved Hitler to do this, instead of landing an army on English shores, may never be clearly stated. Perhaps he decided he could never land that army and so gave up the idea. High government people believed that Hitler decided that it was too costly a project, preferring an attempt to crush England by counter-blockade, combining an attack on shipping with continued bombardment from the air to curtail production. The bombardment, however, did not make the desired inroads on British production.

But we know that at one time Hitler's landing craft were crowded into every French Channel port. It was said that his armies actually took off to test the English defenses, but that the R.A.F. sank thousands of boats filled with fighting men. The fliers did it, according to the gossip, by dropping drums of oil in the Channel near or on the loaded craft as they sailed from the French coasts. The oil was then ignited by flares or incendiaries.

Pat Hurley came back from Russia and told us of Russian resistance. He described one example of that defense—a small city in the line of the German march toward Moscow, where the women from the ages of eight to eighty-five dug a tank-catcher trench twenty feet deep and sixty feet wide completely around the city. Thousands of them dug day and night. As they dug deeper and deeper, they used a ladder formation, the younger women on the bottom handing each shovelful of earth to slightly older women until at the top grandmothers of sixty-five received the dirt and spread it. The whole job was done in ten days. Like China, Russia moved her industry back into the interior. Like China, her people, bleeding at many wounds, stubbornly fought on for their Mother Earth.

Then slyly Japan planted herself down at the lower end of the Asiatic peninsula, where she could attack in three directions: the Philippines, Singapore, and the Burma source of supply for China. She became a daily threat. She was only three hours by bomber from the Philippines. We had tried for two years to appease her. This may have delayed her advance, but it certainly did not prevent it.

We kept on hoping that our tolerant policy would evoke a response from the Japanese people. We thought the Golden Rule was a great working principle of life, as it is if others will respond to it. It worked poorly in this period. In Germany, Italy, and Japan, the Golden Rule was considered a kind of goofy mixture of timidity, weakness and simple-mindedness.

About twenty days before Japan struck Pearl Harbor, Kurusu, the Japanese envoy in Washington, proposed to Secretary Hull that the United States send Japan all the oil she required. Hull approximately answered, "That means you want us to send you oil so you can keep us worried and keep us holding our fleet in the Pacific. You want us to give you the means with which to do it. That is a devil of a proposition!"

Kurusu then asked Mr. Hull to stop all aid to China, to which the Secretary of State retorted, "Why don't you stop helping Hitler?"

Kurusu countered with his repeated offer to get out of Indo-China if and when peace with China was made. Hull said, "That means you are trying to force us to compel China to make peace. Is that all you have to offer?" Kurusu said that it was. Mr. Hull was furious.

After that conference, he reported to the war cabinet that he had done all he could do and that the situation was hopeless. He warned the Army and the Navy to be prepared for surprises, that the Japs would be likely to attack at several places simultaneously, without warning. He had known desperadoes in his Tennessee days, he said. They shoot if sufficiently angered and aroused.

THE DARK DAYS

In OUR HOUSE ON CHAIN BRIDGE ROAD IN Washington, all was gay and happy on December 6, 1941. My eighteen-year-old daughter, Janet, was spending the week-end at home for a change. She had had a very happy girlhood. The constant stream of attractive young men who beaued her every place filled our house with gaiety and youth.

Our guests for this particular week-end were two young seniors from Yale University—fledgling newspapermen. On Saturday night the young people who gathered for cocktails lounged about our house, the boys in fine-tailored, casual suits, and the girls in nifty little numbers which testified to the well-padded pockets of their fathers.

I had a tense argument with one of the boys about the possible entry of the United States into the war. Like so many college boys of the period, he felt that the United States could remain isolationist. It was not that he was afraid, or that he didn't want his young life interrupted by service for his country. It was simply his firm conviction that the United States would be as well off if Germany won the war as it would if Britain won it. Our argument became so impassioned that my embarrassed husband shouted at me to shut up. That broke the tension, and we agreed that this week-end there would be no further discussion of deep political problems.

Sunday, December 7, our house guests all slept late and came down just in time for cocktails before a one-thirty luncheon. We enjoyed the dinner of roast beef and were lingering over coffee and brandy, when my son Peter was called to the telephone. He answered it upstairs because we were laughing and joking so gaily downstairs that he couldn't hear. Suddenly he came falling down the stairs in a great rush, shouting, "Daddy, the Japs have bombed Pearl Harbor!"

I shall never forget that the sentence was not completed before my husband was out the front door and in his car, racing to his office. Almost as quickly, the two young men dashed out of the house and ran down the street. We saw none of them again until about 2 A.M. the next morning. My husband of course was frantically busy at his office and was called upon for radio broadcasts. The two young college newspapermen who had been our guests covered the entire city, too. They saw the Japanese burning their papers and files behind the Japanese Embassy; they witnessed the angry crowds that collected about that embassy; they joined the milling throngs around the White House; and they interviewed every Senator and Cabinet officer they could contact.

The girls and I sat stupefied in front of the radio. We

were so quiet and sorrowful that time and again my little cocker spaniel, Pepper, whimpered and put his head upon my lap, for even he felt the horror that was upon us all. I suppose no person in the United States that day will ever forget exactly where he was, what he was doing, and what he felt when the news of Pearl Harbor hit this country.

I had done my Christmas shopping early and spent the next day trying to wrap the gifts. I couldn't concentrate on even such a trivial task. I would wrap a gift and then forget what was in the package and for whom it was intended. I would unwrap it and start over. I made no attempt to get permission to go up to hear the President's request for a declaration of war from the Congress against the Axis Powers. I was too stunned.

The die was cast and there could be no further argument. In some respects it was a relief to have the issue clearly drawn. We could be proud—proud that we tried to the bitter end to avoid war. We could even be grateful to Japan because she had made our decision for us. We hated war so deeply, were so convinced of its futility as a method of adjusting difficulties, that we were incapable of taking the initiative. Japan gave us unity. All our doubts, all of our reluctance and hesitation, were swept away. The united answer of the country was: Fight!

This was suicide for Japan, a desperate fourth-rate nation, the spoiled little gangster of the Orient. She asked for, and she would be given, extermination as a power. She could have joined the United States and Britain as one of the three controlling sea powers of the world. Her geography and economic situation made that her logical course. An island empire, she could live only by sea trade. She could have avoided war with the United States. Instead, she preferred to take her chances to live by the sword. By so doing, she chose her death by the sword. Blasted, bombed, burned, starved, her people were destined to suffer ghastly tortures.

Westbrook Pegler wrote on December 10: "Ray Clapper was the only cosmic commentator in the trade who really felt the gravity of the Japanese menace to our country. Much of his work on that theme was necessarily pretty dull going, and I will admit to my shame that I sometimes threw Clapper away with the inward remark, 'To Hell, Ray was on tin, rubber, Borneo and the Dutch East Indies again.' . . . Week after week, he hammered on the subject of the Japanese enmity to the United States and the utter ruthlessness of the monkeys of Nippon. . . . To me and to most other Americans who were interested in menaces, Hitler was the one to watch and hate, and the Japanese were just a synthetic danger. . . . The fact that practically all of us were looking the other way, throwing rude monosyllables at Hitler, is certainly no fault of his, because he was on the right track all the time. I am afraid his information was altogether too sound on the subject of our stockpiles of raw materials necessary for war, which were obtainable in quantity only in areas which Japan soon blocked off. . . . Clapper made a campaign of his warnings and the fault was ours that so very few Americans got the message of this press-coop Paul Revere."

The Dark Days

The American public never seemed to comprehend the full threat. We came shudderingly near to defeat the first year we were at war. It was touch-and-go to beat the Germans in North Africa. The Russians barely turned the Germans back at Stalingrad. Japan could have occupied Hawaii and perhaps sections of our west coast.

The average citizen, however, could scarcely believe that our Navy could not sail immediately out into the Pacific for a conclusive showdown with the Japanese navy. But our military leaders knew that until we could throw large numbers of airplanes into the Southwest Pacific the Japanese onrush could not be stopped. For a long time to come, our major concern was concentrated on the Battle of the Atlantic, not the Pacific, and the dispatch of American forces to various parts of the world staggered the imagination. It was the hardest job this nation ever tackled.

In Washington at the center of the effort, we were confused and uncertain. Production lagged. The Capital seethed with feuds and backbiting. The demoralization reached the point, in the early months of 1942, where it interfered with the whole-hearted aggressive prosecution of the war.

Early in January, my husband sought out Bernard Baruch in his room at the Carlton Hotel. Wise old Baruch has contributed much to his country through two wars. He was always popular with newspapermen, who gave him their unqualified support and recognized in him a great organizing genius. He was much more chipper than when Ray had seen him last, the reason being that the President had asked him to turn in a draft plan for reorganizing war production. That day he had just finished the job, the main lines of which were to give Donald Nelson, Executive Director of SPAB, some real power.

When Roosevelt asked Baruch what he thought of Nelson, Baruch answered, "He probably has not done as well as he might have, but to be fair to him, you know, you haven't given him any power."

One of the realities that slowed up the cooperation of business men in the war effort was their fear of being prosecuted under the Sherman Anti-Trust Act. Mr. Baruch told Ray of receiving a letter from the Attorney General, raising the question of anti-trust violations. Baruch telephoned him and told him to lay off, that we had to win a war. First things came first with Baruch. In 1918, during the First World War, business men were in charge and industry had no fear about going ahead into war production.

Mr. Baruch was also critical of Jesse Jones, Secretary of Commerce, who not only had failed to stockpile rubber and other basic materials, but had said that there was no need to rush synthetic production—that everything was going to be all right!

Of great service in pinning down the bungling and delays in war production was the Truman Committee of the Senate. The Truman Reports were encyclopaedia of what was wrong around Washington. You could dip into them at almost any page and be shocked.

Everything seemed dark in those days, yet when President Roosevelt set fantastic goals of production, our industry, our labor and the bureaucracy at Washington met those goals. We accomplished superhuman results, as a free people always can when their energies are unleashed in a task they understand. Perhaps we did it in spite of ourselves, perhaps our natural wealth is of such magnitude we could not fail. Whatever it was—the leadership, the work, the wealth—we turned back the threat. England held, Russia held. Within a year America miraculously had helped to save the world from the fascist triumvirate.

One of the most glamorous visitors who came to Washington in the middle war period was Madame Chiang Kai-shek. She appeared formally before the House of Representatives on Capitol Hill, and in addition she made an informal appearance the same morning before the United States Senate. Senator Alben W. Barkley thoughtfully sent me a ticket of admission to the Senate to see and hear her. I arrived well ahead of the crowd and enjoyed watching all the celebrities of this over-celebrated town arrive. Mrs. Woodrow Wilson, Mrs. Henry Wallace, Mrs. Franklin Roosevelt, and every ambassador, minister, Cabinet officer and member of the Supreme Court were present. Everybody who could beg, borrow, or steal a ticket was there.

At 12:15 P.M., the first lady of China was escorted down the aisle by Senators Barkley, McNary, Caraway, Connally and Capper. In the softest, exquisitely enunciated English, she greeted the Vice President and the Senators. Before the microphone, she began an informal talk, with apologies for her lack of ability in extemporaneous speaking. Gently she told of something she had found in President Roosevelt's library at Hyde Park. "What do you think it was," she asked. "In a glass case I found a first draft, and then a second, and on up to the sixth draft of one of Mr. Roosevelt's speeches. It encouraged me to know that so renowned and excellent a speaker drafts his speeches. When I mentioned it to the President, he said, 'Sometimes I write twelve drafts.'"

Mme. Chiang, in warm, pulsing tones, next told a story about a trip which she and Generalissimo Chiang Kai-shek had taken several months before to the Chinese front. They passed through an ancient Chinese village of two thousand years ago which had been the site of an ancient Buddhist abbey. Its ruins brought back to her mind a two-century-old story of a young Buddhist who was seeking grace. Hour after hour, day after day, month after month, he sat intoning "Buddha, Buddha." One day a very old abbot, watching the young acolyte spending the days of his life so unproductively, started rubbing a brick against a piece of stone. Day after day he too repeated this process, until finally the young novice asked him, "Why do you rub that brick against that piece of stone?"

The abbot replied, "I am trying to make a mirror."

The young novice was astonished, and said, "But, Father, you cannot make a mirror that way."

To which the old abbot replied, "No more can you acquire

grace by sitting there day after day intoning 'Buddha, Buddha.' "

It was a simple little story, from which Mme. Chiang pointed out that fine sentiments and grand words could not bring us into a post-war world of peace and plenty unless the people of the United Nations took steps to bring about that world by joining together in a definite program, not at some future date but immediately.

Unforgettable also was the press conference that she held jointly with President Roosevelt. It was high state drama, played by real characters. It was the delicate, feminine, shrewd, witty and powerful first lady of China, against the great master dramatist himself, Franklin D. Roosevelt. As the press conference began, the President asked the reporters not to put any catchy questions to Madame. She in turn played to the President as the big strong man who could work miracles. Mme. Chiang, with feet dangling from the high-seated chair, toyed with her compact, but worked smoothly to coax a promise out of President Roosevelt for China. He was trying with equal smoothness not to melt too much under Madame's technique. It was a great show. Two hundred reporters watched Mme. Chiang give a lively little greeting with delicate prose flowers to everyone. She sat between the President and Mrs. Roosevelt, who laid her hand protectingly on Madame's fragile arm.

A reporter thrust a direct question, as to whether China's manpower was being fully used in the war. Madame held her poise, but replied that China's men were fighting wherever and whenever munitions were available to them. She said that when more munitions were sent to China, more men would fight.

With such a finesse, she threw the ball squarely into the lap of the President. He explained, rather sheepishly, that we would send munitions as fast as the Lord would let us. Then Madame, smiling so politely and sweetly, tossed the ball for a goal when she murmured that the Lord helps those who help themselves.

That was the moment at which President Roosevelt indicated that the conference had gone on long enough, and as the reporters left the room, the three great actors sat inscrutably in a neat row. Mrs. Roosevelt's hand was no longer protectingly laid on Madame's arm. Not a hair ruffled, Madame gazed impersonally and imperturbably in front of her. She had done a job for China.

Chapter Seventeen

RENDEZVOUS
OF THREE MEN

IT IS NOT MY PURPOSE TO FIGHT THE WAR
all over again. Our Army, Navy, Marine Corps, and Air
Force have done their job so admirably that it is presumptu-
ous for a civilian to do anything except express gratitude.
Never before in our history were greater feats of courage
and sacrifice performed. This "soft" generation about which
we fretted in the 1930's has sinews of steel and stout hearts.
We can be proud of them.

Twelve years after the Nazis came to power in Germany
—a power that Hitler said would last a thousand years—
Germany lay completely crushed. The Japanese Empire
lasted less than four months longer. To the victors there were
no spoils, only the strange paradox of having to shoulder
burdens of mass starvation and ruin amid the disintegration
of much of the world. If any part of civilization was to be
saved it was more necessary for the Allies to work together
in the post-war era than in the war.

With the defeat of Germany, May 7, 1945, and of Japan,
August 14, 1945, it became evident that two giant powers

had emerged—Russia and the United States. The people of the United States became more than ever preoccupied with our relations with the Soviet Union as a possible political, economic, and military rival. Some of us believed that we could get along amicably with this new Goliath; others saw inevitable clashes leading to another war.

Ray and I spent a little time in Russia in 1937. The mystery that was Russia, added to the phenomena of the Soviet regime, was unfathomable to us. We found much fear and suspicion. Foreigners knew that in every room the Soviets had dictaphones concealed in the walls recording conversations. To break these recordings, you continually rapped on a glass or a table. You got quickly into the habit of going for walks if you wanted to have a conversation unmarred by eavesdroppers. Every place we went a secret police agent followed close behind. That was a protection in reality, because it was difficult to get lost or into much trouble with our "shadow" close to us.

We had a list of Russians—friends of Americans who had worked in Russia. We had hoped to visit and talk with these Russians. But when we learned the danger in which our visit would put them, we burned the list in order that no suspicion of fraternization with foreigners could touch them.

In order to pick up crumbs of knowledge about the rising Russian Bear we were limited for the most part to discussions with American and British diplomats and newspaper correspondents. We saw millions of the population at work and at play, chewing and spitting the sunflower seeds they love; but our dream of understanding and knowing the Russian people and their government was unfulfilled.

Moscow was a thriving place three hundred years before Columbus discovered America. This heavy crust of ancient civilization was the Soviets' most formidable enemy. They had the task of converting a medieval peasant people into a modern, skilled, industrial nation in one generation. It was a high-pressure effort, rough and brutal. It was the most monumental bootstrap experiment in history.

Our own struggle to conquer the West was turbulent and ruthless. Like our pioneers, the Russians were struggling to subdue a continent, larger than ours and equally rich in natural resources. The Russians were compelled to conquer nature and an enemy more entrenched than were our Indian tribes—ancient habits, prejudices, extreme ignorance, and poverty, all centuries old. And at the same time, they felt the bitter enmity of a whole world, never knowing from whence or at what moment attack would come.

We saw some of the newer apartment buildings in factory sections. Once, accompanied by an interpreter, we knocked on an apartment door. The grandmother of the family, a toothless old woman, opened the door. She was cordial, ushered us into a comfortable living room where her granddaughter sat at a piano in the middle of a music lesson. The family had four rooms, two of which were bedrooms, a gas stove in the kitchen, a radio, a dog, and a cat. Geraniums bloomed in the curtained windows. The father of this family was a dispatcher in a factory, earning eight hundred rubles a month; the mother was a supervisor of nursery work, earning five hundred rubles a month. Together, they earned about $260 in American money. That was high pay, the average being more nearly two hundred and thirty-one rubles a month. The comparative figure meant nothing, however, as the ruble was trick currency, having no relation in buying power to dollars.

This family must have been in extraordinarily good party standing to have enjoyed so much housing room. The criterion of aristocracy and privilege in Russia was good housing and food privileges, in contrast to the money criterion in the United States. So severe was the shortage of rooms in Moscow that most families could secure only a curtained-off part of a room and, consequently, knew little privacy. Moscow was a city of four million, but it had housing for only 800,000. As the Soviets accelerated their building program, whole sections of the city were being torn down, subways built, great beautiful avenues laid out which some day will make it a handsome city. With a rush Moscow blasted and rebuilt, while her people in patient faith lived as best they could.

On the outskirts, we visited primitive individual homes where conditions were frightful. The floors were the earth itself; everything was slovenly and filthy beyond belief. One hut, no larger than an American kitchen, housed two families. The walls were only boards without plaster or paper; there was no heat, no bed, and not even a "Chic Sale."

Out of this household, two boys and one husband had gone into the Red Army.

As in America, there were wide variations in living standards. The worst sections were not much worse than slums in our own cities, but the best fell several notches below the standards of workmen in America. This was because of the high cost of clothing and the shortages of consumer goods.

Stalin, as the name suggests, was a man of hard, steely temperament, inclined to be inarticulate and therefore impatient of dialecticians and theorists. He was disposed to make short work of such people. A phrase of his, hanging on a sign in the office of the newspaper *Pravda*, was significant: "Talk Less and Work More."

Stalin, driving ruthlessly toward expanding production, building up the army, making Russia powerfully self-sufficient, swept aside without batting an eye anything that seemed to him to stand in the way. He was an efficient man and a builder, not a theorist. Life was cheap, and the place for political critics was in prison or under the sod. Stalin put them where they couldn't talk back.

These purges, demoralizing industry by creating widespread fear and terror among executives all the way down the line, appeared nevertheless to have increased Stalin's strength rather than damaged it. He not only removed many critics and incompetents, but he also appeased the feelings of the rank and file who, struggling hard themselves, had seen incompetent superiors enjoying many special privileges. The worker felt that Stalin was fighting *his* battle by removing incompetent and plotting superiors. The rank and file read only what the regime wanted them to read, and they knew only that much.

The purges strengthened Stalin's grip on the Soviet Union. Make no mistake, Stalin was in the driver's seat. His team stumbled a little and made slow progress over the bumps, but he gritted his teeth and lashed it on up the hill.

The greatest achievement of Soviet Russia was the Red Army. For it, everything else had been subordinated. The workers went poorly clad because so much went into army uniforms. If there was a shortage of nails for Moscow carpenters, no one was too deeply concerned; but let there be any anxiety over aviation equipment or radio communication and a hurry call would be sent for foreign technical assistance.

The result was an army that has made the Soviet Union one of the leading world powers and probably the strongest of the continental powers. Information that we regarded as reliable placed the first-line strength of the Soviet Army in 1937 at 1,400,000 men and its trained reservists at a minimum of 4,000,000—making in all 5,400,000 men trained to take the field upon call. Behind these were 12,000,000 untrained men of military age, for the Russian population was so large that only one youth out of four or five was conscripted.

Industrially, the Soviet Union was still in a primitive stage. Until the oncoming generation could be thoroughly trained in workmanship, industrial maturity was a considerable distance in the future. The Soviet system operated, down to the last minor individual unit, from a central control tower. We questioned whether such a vast mechanism could be managed by the small group at the top. One virtue of capitalism is that it is self-motivating and self-controlling. The absolute and all-powerful dictatorship brushed aside the new Constitution—carrying guarantees of personal liberty similar to ours.

We left Russia feeling that Stalin's hope was based on the youth of the nation. If they could escape the curse of old national habits, learn the use of modern tools, learn modern administrative technique, find ways of functioning without terrorism, then in the years to come we'd see one of the greatest civilizations of all time. If they failed, a monumental tragedy was in store for the world.

As we passed over the border back into Poland, we couldn't resist waving to our "shadow," who stood immobile, frowning, on the tracks. He had never spoken to us; he did not wave to us as we laughingly waved good-bye to him.

Our brief experience in Soviet Russia did give us a slight comprehension of the baffling Russian temperament. When the war came we could understand the struggles of Roosevelt and Churchill to work with Stalin. Russia was the key to Europe. What did she want?

Urgent decisions needed to be made for waging the war. Even more urgent agreements were needed on post-war aims. Yet Stalin played a lone hand. He would not confer. He stuck to his oft-repeated excuse that he could not leave his country for a conference in the midst of his military campaign.

Roosevelt declared privately that he would do anything to bring about a conference, even if he had to swallow his pride and go to Moscow. He felt it was imperative to know Stalin's ideas about Germany after her defeat, for if Germany should suddenly collapse the Big Three had no correlated program.

Equally important to know were the Soviets' territorial demands. What would they settle for? Obviously Russia would insist that the Baltic States—Latvia, Esthonia, and Lithuania—should become Russian. But would she expect a large slice of Eastern and Central Europe from the Baltic to the Black Sea—Poland, Roumania, Yugoslavia, maybe Greece? If so, what would be the effect of such demands upon America and Britain?

Throughout the war the Russians were so close-mouthed that we didn't know how strong their army really was, what reserves they had, or how well-equipped they were in fighting the Germans. Our observers were not permitted to observe anything. We sent the Soviets millions in Lend-Lease but they never acknowledged publicly that we were taking any weight off their battle front. In private messages, however, they admitted that we had relieved them of much of their supply burdens.

For a man of his impetuous disposition, President Roosevelt showed extraordinary patience with what he called "the Russian way." He said, "They don't throw their hats up in the air in appreciation of what we have done, but that doesn't mean they lack gratitude. Sometimes when you least expect them to understand a move they surprise you by agreeableness."

An instance of this was the time German submarines in the Murmansk shipping lanes were sinking 50 percent of our ships. We had to quit shipping on that route for a time. When the bad news was broken to Stalin he agreed and understood even though this was the only sea route to Russia.

Roosevelt also showed firmness with Russia. He halted, by his own personal intervention, a diplomatic move between Great Britain and the Soviet Union that, had it come to fruition, might have cost all of us many allies in the war, in addition to being a serious psychological handicap. The Soviets asked Great Britain in January, 1942, to sign a treaty with them allowing Russia large territorial gains in Europe after the war. At this particular time the British people had just undergone months of frightful German blitz. They knew what the Russian people were going through as the Germans swept across toward Stalingrad. They felt deep kinship and appreciation because the Russians had lifted the awful pressure off them. They were ready to agree to anything the Russians asked.

However, Anthony Eden, British Secretary of Foreign Affairs, was not too eager to accede to all the demands. He offered a substitute treaty of friendship for 20 years between the two nations.

When the Russians refused that treaty, the British cabinet, spurred by British public opinion, was all set to approve the territorial draft. It was scheduled for a Cabinet meeting one Friday morning. Roosevelt was deeply disturbed when he heard. He well knew the effect of such an agreement on American public opinion. We had been in the war only one month. He instructed our Ambassador to Great Britain, John Winant, to do everything possible to block the agreement.

Winant moved fast. It was Thursday. Through Russian Ambassador Maisky in London he requested an appointment that day to talk with Soviet Foreign Minister Molotov, who was in London. That was impossible, Molotov said; how about luncheon next Tuesday? Winant knew that would be too late. He made his request stronger. He must see Molotov that Thursday night, he said, on a matter of urgent concern to the United States and Russia. Finally Maisky gave in and 10 P.M. that night was set.

Winant spent one hour and fifteen minutes with Molotov. When he opened his conversation with the Russian he said he wanted to "talk turkey." The interpreter thought he meant Winant wanted to talk about Turkey. It took ten minutes for Winant to make clear what "talk turkey" meant in American idiom. He turned it into an amusing incident which broke the ice.

Winant's argument was basically on the line that public opinion in the United States was quite different from British public opinion in regard to these claims of Russia. In Britain, the people's friendliness for Russia was far ahead of the government's in wanting to help Russia, but in America, the government was ahead of the public in understanding these claims. He told Molotov that Russia's best friends in Washington were bitterly opposed to recognizing Russian territorial demands and that insistence on this treaty would create the most serious embarrassment for the United States Government. Winant talked long and convincingly. At 11:15 P.M. Molotov interrupted to say, "We will substitute the Eden agreement for the treaty we had intended to sign. You can tell your government we will not insist on the territorial treaty." Winant felt that was a good moment to leave. He quickly departed.

When much later it became clear that the Baltic States would inevitably become Russian, President Roosevelt hoped some way could be found to protect the minorities there. He feared that the treatment of individual dissenters would be ruthless and suggested that some arrangement be made whereby those who wanted to leave those areas under Russian control could take their movable property and leave. He was not able to do this, of course.

An interesting sidelight on Franklin Roosevelt at this time came at an off-the-record press conference. Questioned about Russia's demands to include Latvia, Esthonia, and Lithuania in the Soviet Union, he said, "Well, they are destined to become Russian. Obviously I am not going to fight Russia for the Baltic States." Newspapermen wondered if his continued power was going to his head so that he used the kingly pronoun "I" instead of the usual "we."

Rendezvous of Three Men

When, after one and a half years, all efforts to arrange a conference between the Big Three leaders had failed, the situation between them was tense in March, 1943. For good or bad reasons, Stalin could not be induced to meet with the other two. Harry Hopkins had been devoting much time to arranging a meeting.

Perhaps Sumner Welles was right when he told Ray that the trouble might be traced to Russia's uncertainty as to what America intended to do. Perhaps Stalin would not act so coy if he were sure that we would stay in the war. Not knowing us well, he thought we might back out when the going got rough. In such a case, he wondered if Britain might team up with Germany against Russia. Again Stalin did not understand the Anglo-Saxon mind. He tried to secure Russia against any and all treacherous possibilities.

Finally in the spring of 1943 the President sent Joe Davies to Moscow because he seemed to get along with Stalin. He persuaded Stalin to set the date of a meeting—August 1, 1943. As to the place of meeting, Stalin promised to let Roosevelt know by July 10. But July 10 to 15 went by with no word. Plans for the Quebec meeting with Churchill had by that time come up and Roosevelt cabled Stalin. A reply from Moscow came, saying Stalin was at the war front and was unable to communicate. Roosevelt was a little incredulous that there were no communication facilities at the Russian front. Finally, however, from Moscow Stalin sent word it was impossible for him to get away.

Churchill bitterly described this as a run-around but

Roosevelt felt it only illustrated the unpredictability of the Russians.

Of course eventually the three leaders did meet at Teheran in November, 1943, and the understandings reached could be carried over successfully into the post-war period. Sumner Welles was undoubtedly right. Once the Russians found they could trust us and the British, they were willing in their fashion to go 50 percent toward cooperation.

At the opening session in the Russian Embassy at Teheran, Roosevelt and Churchill waited for Stalin, the host, to open the meeting. Stalin sat silent, looking much like a country lad just arrived in the big city, wearing a strange iridescent uniform out of cloth especially woven for him. Roosevelt, unable to endure the embarrassing minutes ticking away, broke the ice by a few extemporaneous remarks to the effect that this was an historic moment, that the destiny of the world depended upon the decisions they were about to make and added other flowery observations. Again there was silence. Then Churchill took up the conversation, throwing a small bouquet of oratory. Silence once more. All looked at Stalin, who finally cryptically said, "The sentiments are very appropriate. I agree with them. Let's get down to business."

He wanted victory over Germany at the earliest possible moment because, he said, the Russian people were taking such terrible punishment. He wanted all the good things of life for them, the same as other civilized people had. In no instance did he ever indicate a desire to occupy any large part of Europe. Rather he seemed like a father holding the single idea of providing well for his children.

Often the British and ourselves do not understand Soviet procedure, nor do they understand ours. Anthony Eden had a painful example of this when he was in Moscow in 1942. Stalin shoved at him a draft of a treaty, asking him to sign it then and there. Eden explained that he had no authority from the British Government to sign a treaty, that it had to be referred to the Cabinet, the Dominions, et cetera. He offered to initial it to show his own personal approval and promised to take it back to London for consideration. Returning the next day to see Stalin, he found him angry and sour. In blunt language Stalin said, "Yesterday you said you could not sign a treaty. I have found you signed one with Turkey."

Eden explained that the Turkish treaty was the result of long negotiations and had been duly authorized. Upon this explanation Stalin subsided.

It is as hard for us to understand the Russians as it is for them to understand us. Secretary Hull confessed to my husband after he returned from his epochal trip to Moscow late in 1943 that he had no idea when he left Washington whether the Russians intended to go isolationist after the war or would join the other nations in a security program. If they went isolationist, he believed anarchy would prevail in the world and another world war would be unavoidable. He intended to do his utmost to prevent such a catastrophe. Without consulting his wife or his physician, he flew halfway round the world on a hazardous trip, at the age of seventy-two. When he arrived, Stalin and Molotov could not have been more cordial. There was considerable exchange of information of all kinds, and, most important of all, arrangements were made for continuous contact between the three governments as equal partners.

Donald Nelson also went to Russia and he, like Wendell Willkie, was much impressed with their cordiality and their production job. All their war plants were opened for him to see. He was lavishly entertained at dinners by commissars living in palatial splendor. One Russian host exuberantly honoring Nelson dashed a fine dinner plate on the floor to prove his admiration. Nelson, not to be outdone, smashed two more, cutting his hand badly. This gallantry impressed the Russians enormously.

When Nelson met Stalin, he explained that he was a business man, not a politician. Stalin said, "I don't like politicians either." Nelson complimented Stalin on the magnificent war achievement of the Red Army. Stalin replied, "They ought to be good now because we have made every mistake it is possible for us to make."

Donald Nelson may have struck the key upon which the Soviet Union and the United States can get along when he told a Communist Party official in Siberia that the United States should not try to interfere with Russia or Russia with the United States. He suggested that for the next twenty years or so there probably would be socialist competition with

American capitalism. In such a contest we would see which system was best. The Russians liked such forthrightness.

He brought home a picture of Russia's turning ideologically to the right. In a sense, their industry is more competitive than ours. Not only is there intense rivalry between plants, but there is greater competition among the individual workers in contrast to our trade-union methods of uniform output per man. They reward all who find ways to produce more goods; the harder a man works the more honor he gets.

Mr. Nelson found, as we did, that there was little of the "common level" association that we tend to think of as typically Soviet between plant managers and workers. Personal attitudes are friendly, but class differences are developing. The young managers have not worked up from the bench or forge. They have been educated and trained to be managers. They own automobiles and often have several servants in their homes. Curiously enough a person's social station in life is fairly well indicated by the quality of shoes he wears. Those of the plant managers are very good indeed.

Many business men here believe that the United States and Russia can trade together after the war, that the two countries can profit by an exchange of the things each needs. Russia needs capital goods—ten thousand locomotives, thirty thousand freight cars, thousands of kilometers of rails and machine tools of all kinds. We, on the other hand, need some raw materials which have been depleted by the war—high-grade copper, molybdenum, industrial diamonds, oil. We could use furs and lumber too. The two countries are in a position to be thoroughly complementary to each other for many years.

Learning to get along with our British allies was much simpler than with the Soviet Union. A common language, a similar form of government, a common denominator of standards of all kinds helped mutual understanding. There was an argument about the cross-Channel attack on Europe. Churchill did not want to sacrifice any more British lives, he was fearful of heavy casualties that would for a second generation kill off the majority of England's best young men. He wanted the attack postponed as long as possible and a 50-50 proportion of British and American troops. In the end, the percentage of Americans participating was much greater.

The chief differences, however, between Churchill and Roosevelt were over post-war plans for colonies and trusteeships. Churchill was a complete Tory and would not discuss any change. Gossip around Washington hinted that on over-all post-war policies, the United States found it easier to deal with Stalin and Generalissimo Chiang than with Churchill.

When all was said and done, the circumstances that made us joint operators in the war, give us joint interests in the future world. If we break apart at any point we are each the weaker. We have always had a traditional fear of being outsmarted by the British, of thinking they were using us. It should be the other way around. They needed us and always had to be fearful that we would run out on them as we did after World War I. Together after this war we will have all the navy that exists in the world. With Russia added, the three of us have all the air power. But it is the United States who holds all the chips. Poker is an American institution.

Looking into the future of our foreign relations for a moment, we have two needs. One is the imperative necessity for a long-range basic policy that will develop regardless of what political party is in power, and extending into generations to come. Its roots must be deep and as devoted to the welfare of our people as is the Russian or the British policy. Obviously it will stress continuous cooperation with the other nations in this close-knit world.

The other need is for abler men, for trained men skilled in the techniques of world affairs. The British and the Russians always seem to have better trained men than ours for these specific jobs. We can afford to lift our qualifications out of the political ward heeler's class. Such men are not good enough any longer.

We come to the end of the Roosevelt era. Both V-E day and V-J day were fitting memorials to his genius. We know now that he was no dictator. The fact that after his death the wheels of government went on turning without hesitation, that the Pacific war was brought to a rapid, successful finish, that the Congress and the people rallied behind still another able President, proves beyond a doubt the good health of our democracy.

Rendezvous of Three Men

We face two basic issues. First, what is the responsibility of the United States in the world of jealous sovereign nations who face the implications of an atomic age? Second, can private capitalism function as it has in the past, or must the federal government interfere as democratically as possible to assist in providing a good life for all our people, regardless of race or color?

The answers to these two questions are still in the future. We will worry a lot and we will struggle. But the issues have been spelled out for us in the past twenty-five years. We recognize them now as old enemies—war and poverty. Two generations have been required to fight, bleed, and die in order to teach us that we could, if we would, defeat these two deadly foes. To do it we need head-work, not emotions and prejudices.

This post-war generation, having proved its valiance in battle, knows no fear. It is strong and unprejudiced. The world must be made more nearly into the image our young men and women visualized as they fought. This is a debt owed to the dead as well as to the living.

We have exciting work to do—challenging work as important as winning the war. The reward is ever greater riches, both material and spiritual. We can accomplish this work. We have the wealth and we have the leadership. Still more important we have a nation of people full of common sense. They will find the tools and the methods. What is more they will have an exciting, interesting time doing it.

I wish Raymond Clapper could watch them do it.